D1387128

LAKELAND YESTERDAY

VOLUME II

For Ross and Josie.

LAKELAND YESTERDAY
VOLUME II

Irvine Hunt

Waltersgill

First published in 2011 by
Waltersgill
Photography & Publishing,
17 Wrenbeck Drive, Otley,
West Yorkshire, LS21 2BP.

Paperback ISBN 978 0 9556454 2 6

Hardback ISBN 978 0 9556454 3 3

Printed and bound by
Smith Settle
Gateway Drive, Yeadon,
West Yorkshire, LS19 7XY.

Contents

Introduction

IN THE HEART OF the English Lake District, a few miles from a popular holiday town yet attracting no special attention from the many passers-by, there is a fine but modest-sized house with a well-cared-for garden and the kind of glorious view of the mountains that many of us would delight in as we stepped out of our door each morning: Lakeland at its most beautiful.

And all seems innocent enough, yet there is in fact more to this pleasant-looking house than that, for nearby, and seemingly still unsuspected by most passers-by, there is a kind of hidden treasure, one that was buried many years ago in among the bushes, or perhaps under one of the pleasant stretches of lawn that make up the gardens. And while there are people who say they have heard of the existence of the hoard, and some that they know about the time that it was buried, no one has claimed publicly to have found it, though stories exist that a few keen-eyed people armed with spades have certainly looked.

This treasure is not made up of money or jewels and such, but comprises of a large collection of half- and probably whole-plate glass photographic negatives, many hundreds of pictures of the old days, the exact nature of which no one is quite certain, but probably of stagecoaches, steamers and trains, cars struggling over the mountain passes, men and women on cycles, portraits and possibly much more. A photographic hoard. Indeed, the number can only be guessed at.

They were buried a long time ago by a once well-known Lakeland photographer who had decided to call it a day and had moved to the old house in quiet retirement. With him went the mass of glass negatives, at that time in good order, but apparently, so the story goes, just too much lumber for the old man to want around in his old age, too much to keep stored on shelves gathering the dust. The photographer decided to be rid of all the glass and, assisted by a home help, they dug pits in the garden and buried the lot, thinking that there would never be cause to disturb them again. And there it seems that the phantom glass remains to this day, for it is fairly certain that, had it come to light in modern times, then a new flood of old photographs, however damaged the emulsion might be during all the years, would be going the rounds with all the attendant stories about their rescue, an event perhaps to equal an auction which took place in Keswick years ago of a large collection of photographs by well-known Lakeland photographer brothers, a collection which manly remember as historical treasure indeed.

The present book, the fifth and final one of a set that began with *The Lakeland Pedlar*, does not, as far as is known, contain any of the lost hoard from the old house, for it has been made possible in the main by the kindness of many private people who have generously and enthusiastically lent their heirlooms for copying and use here.

A number of the photographs are published for the first time, coming from family albums.

Is it Only …

Is it only 120 years or so ago that grandmothers, mothers and their children lined up in Penrith at the public wash-house, waiting to do the weekly wash . . .

A hundred years ago, when these boys in Rusland Valley earned a shilling a week stripping trees of their bark for the tanneries . . .

Only 1908 that the first car in Sawrey was this Argyll, driven by chauffeur Bruce Dixon for Mr Buxton of Beach Mount . . .

Only 1929 when these men and women crowded Main Street, Cockermouth — with a straw in their caps or lips to show that they were for hire . . .

Still the 1920's, that men and women crawled for miles through the fields on hands and knees weeding the turnips . . .

No guesses as to how many years ago it was when this daredevil rider set off up a Lakeland mountainside on his motorcycle – and hopefully got to the top. The temptation is to say that really it is just a clever case of camera tilt, and that is what it might be, except that there are plenty of young bloods around today who do just this very same thing.

Plenty of Dust, Plenty of Mud

MANY CUMBRIAN ROADS a century ago were little better than rough country lanes or tracks. One traditional method to repair them was to tumble a cartload of stones into the biggest holes, and leave the traffic to help flatten out the heaps.

In hot weather on horse routes, as in Furness, the roads were sometimes too thick in dust even to ride a bike. Cottagers saved washing-up water and tea leaves to dampen the road down at their doors. There was a good side, though, for when the wind blew the dust into the fields it was worth a guinea a peck, that was the saying. In bad weather, of course, there was plenty of mud.

Some Lakeland roads were devils to build. A good one straddles Honister Pass these days, and though steep it is mostly taken for granted. Modern cars speed over so easily that we tend to forget what an impressive job it was, what a hard task the road builders had.

Besides road builders, here too is a wide range in transport, from a wondrous Sociable Tricycle to car drivers boldly tackling the mountain passes, from waterplanes struggling to lift off Windermere, to the men who pioneered the early bus routes, when grass still grew in the middle of the roads.

Opposite:
Under the watchful eye of Mr Kirsopp, road surveyor, on the right, workmen repair Alston's stone sett road. In time, lower down, part was to be treated with tarmacadam, but a century ago the bumpy ride lasted most of the way down through the town. From the left, the boys are Charles and Jack Simpson with their dog; Albert Walton; in stylish pose, John Millican, whose draper's shop is nearby; an unknown roadman; bearded Mr Martin, foreman; and Mr Kirsopp.

A Lakeland stone-breaker in a roadside quarry, when a sixty-hour or even longer working week was the case. Men like this fellow in High Furness used to sit on folded sacking, their legs protected by wrapping bags as they hammered away at stone for the roads. Once the stones were broken, they were piled into long oblong stacks, flat on top, and the knapper was paid by the cubic yard which the foreman measured with his ruler. In 1900 a knapper's weekly wage was about sixteen shillings.

Facing page:
A road takes shape: Honister Pass under reconstruction, 1934-5. It twists down through a valley of stones, the roadrollers struggling to work on the steep slopes, a bleak route through the mountains. The contract was advertised by Cumberland County Council, but there was no rush to take on the job. The harshness that was Honister was well known — unpredictable weather, hairpin bends, one-in-four bits, and a rough, deeply grooved track, parts of which were used by traffic from the slate quarry at the top of the pass. The job went to Henry and William Dowthwaite of Skelton, who were said to be the only contractors in the North-West willing to take on the task. The Dowthwaites and their workmen started in fine enough weather, but a grim winter ensued, with seemingly endless wind, rain, hail and snow. Honister, William used to remark wryly, was the hardest job he ever did in the whole of his life.

Honister Pass was just too steep for a steamroller to work efficiently by itself, so Henry Dowthwaite and his son William did not risk a runaway, but ingeniously anchored the lower machine by a steel cable and winched it up and down. The cable linking the two Aveling and Porter rollers is hard to see, but it is there.

A steamroller in trouble. This Aveling and Porter had been flattening a road in the wilds of Newlands Valley when it crossed a section undermined by a beck. The driver, one Willie Simpson of Cleator Moor, leapt for his life as the road collapsed, taking the roller with it. Willie escaped unhurt. The fallen roller at Newlands was saved by farming contractor Henry Dowthwaite of Skelton and Stalker Brothers of Penrith. They pulled it upright with a cable latched to a threshing engine. Stalkers repaired the machine and it went back into service.

The machine was owned by William Charles Sutton of Beckermet. It was a real family firm. William started threshing and road-mending in 1918, with a second-hand roller bought for £200. With his sons Sidney and Charlie, he built up a successful business, working for different councils ranging from Millom to Cockermouth. Father and sons bought more rollers until they had a fleet of seven, all second-hand, all trusty Aveling and Porters. Suttons' business was sold in the 1950s. Two rollers went to Hexham; others went as scrap, but the one that took the plunge at Newlands went to a jam factory in Maryport and was used to flatten old jam tins.

Opposite top: One of the great sights used to be the stagecoaches clattering along Lakeland's old roads. And there were plenty of them. Here a coach and four from Keswick pauses outside the Prince of Wales, Grasmere, before continuing to Ambleside. Many hotels provided their own transport, for it was often a case of meeting guests as well as taking them back to their trains. The Prince of Wales and the Rothay hotels used to keep more than a hundred horses.

Below: Lakeland's stagecoaches were even celebrated in pianoforte pieces. Various versions of the cover seem to have existed. This one depicts Tom Fidler and passengers outside Wythburn Church. For nearly thirty years Tom drove the 10:48am coach from Windermere Station through Grasmere and on to Keswick, and locals swore you could set your watch by Tom, he was so punctual.

If horses were important in road transport, they were even more important on the land. Here three Clydesdales, bred for strength, make their mark at Low Plains, Calthwaite, the men and beasts paying little attention to the Fordson tractor that is trailing them. The picture is an exception to the general period of this book, but significant for it sharply illustrates the looming change-over of a centuries-old tradition. It is the 1940s and farmer Ernie Threlkeld of Scales Farm, Mungrisdale, is out in front with a favourite team, Darkie, Tommy and Jewel, ploughing ready for planting potatoes. There seemed no greater joy than a team of willing horses pulling well. Two other horses are following on and, last in line, are Jack and Alan Threlkeld with the Fordson.

The horse was still the most useful animal on Lakeland farms and the slow pattern of the plough seemed set to go on at the same steady pace, just as in past centuries. But of course that was not to be. The looming war years of 1939-45, especially towards the end, would see the emergence of the tractor in its thousands and the horse near enough finished for farm work.

The Threlkeld family — which can trace its history in Lakeland back 600 years for sure, but possible even 800 years — switched to the new motor power, just like the rest of the farming community, for however much a man might admire a horse, there was no denying the speed and superior strength of the new machines. No denying, also, that the change-over was often painful. Many a farmworker felt broken hearted as the Darkies, Tommys and the Jewels of this world were sold off, often to the knackers' yards.

The road along Borrowdale Valley has a rough and dusty look about it, and just the one vehicle in sight. This three-horse wagon, a kind of local bus, is well loaded. It has a slightly funereal air, but perhaps it was just carrying the valley folk on a Keswick shopping outing. The valley for long enjoyed a reputation for remoteness, and the wits claim that the wheel arrived in Cumbria long after it had arrived elsewhere. In Borrowdale's case, not until as late as 1824 was it recorded that a chaise driven by a Mr Jack Cawx was the first to penetrate the valley.

The start of a cycle race in Main Street, Cockermouth, 1893. The bicycle craze of the 1890s was under way and where better to begin a grand event than at the foot of the town's distinctive clock, known locally as Neddy. Uniformed soldiers, farmhands, lassies in long dresses, and the lads and men in caps, boaters and hard hats. It was a magnetic occasion for anyone lucky enough to own a bike, and many wanted to.

The coming of the cycle gave people considerable mobility and was of great social significance. For women especially it was seen as a liberating machine and they were often shown in bicycle posters as having been freed and feminine. With their bikes, Cumbria's hired hands found it easier to take up longer-range jobs, increasing the possibility of better-paid work. Even the chances of courting couples were improved. At Dunmail Raise, an old farmhand related how as a young man he regularly courted a girl at Mungrisdale, took her to Saturday dances at Mosedale and cycled back to his workplace by night, a round trip of some thirty-five miles (55km). Others have told of similar amorous journeys.

The rapid spread of cycling was an impressive development. In England in 1885 some 200 firms were making Ordinaries, as they were called — popularly nicknamed Penny Farthings — and there were more than 400,000 cyclists. The machines, with their solid tyres, could travel at 20mph (32kmh) or so over the rough roads. Some weighed up to 60 lb (27kg), though racing models were below 30 lb (13.5kg), including aluminium ones at 20 lb (9kg). While 1872-3 is said to mark the start of the modern cycle, it was about 1891 that saw the beginning of the bicycle's real popularity. Fierce competition developed among firms in the 1890s to sell machines. At Grasmere Sports in 1903, cyclists were described as 'that large class of modern travellers', as indeed they were. In 1895, there were 1,200 cycle clubs in England alone.

Big cycling clubs often had uniforms in green, grey or black. Many at the start of the last century had buglers who blew lustily when it was time to mount, or to stop for lunch. They also had a captain or sub-captain whose word was law. In the Barrow Central Wheelers, for instance, a member was not allowed to pass a captain on a club run. If anyone did, they were brought up before a committee and probably fined one penny.

Back in Cockermouth, the clock was in memory of Edward Waugh, last representative of Parliament of the ancient borough. It was put up by public subscription and became the centrepiece at New Year celebrations. Neddy was removed in the 1930s.

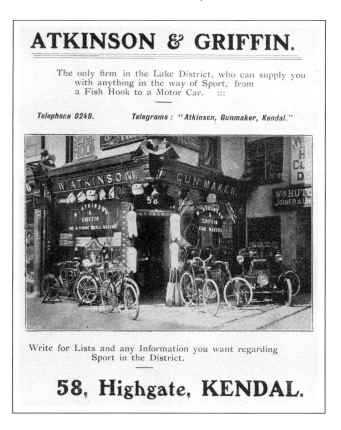

Alston Cycling Club all set for a spin in the 1880s. The men proudly display their cycling club caps, while the women sit on their tricycles rather more smartly dressed than their companions. Tricycles were popular with women, who were able to wear skirts which modestly covered their legs and ankles, yet still allowed them to enjoy the freedom afforded by their daring, adventurous machines. Queen Victoria had a tricycle and that helped to popularise them for women in general. On the left are two advanced cross-framed safety bikes. All the machines have solid tyres, though none as yet has gears. The club was photographed at the bottom of North Lonning outside Lonning Foot House.

Fancy beard, fancy clothes ... if the rider is elaborately dressed, his machine is plain enough, propped up discretely on the handle of a pickaxe. This solid boneshaker was in use at Cark in Cartmel.

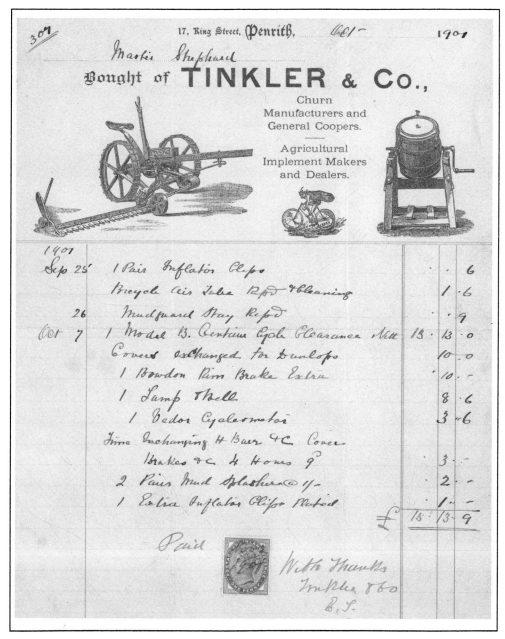

Old billheads can tell their own story, as in this example for Master Shephard in 1901. Churns and mowers were not the only items to be had at Tinklers in Penrith, for bicycles likewise were part of their business. Master Shephard seems to have had all the pleasure that goes with buying a new machine: exchanging the tyre covers for Dunlops; a new bell to warn pedestrians and horses that he was around; and a new lamp (usually these were carbide, primed by water and lit with a match). The first three items on the bill suggest that an older machine was being repaired. Perhaps buying a new one arose out of useful visits to the repairers by Master Shephard with his dad. It's always worth a try.

Both hands are firmly on the steering, and perhaps that is just as well when such a neat-waisted girl is sitting so closely alongside. This wonderful machine is a Sociable Tricycle and made eyes turn whenever it appeared on the roads at Millom.

Their bikes garlanded in flowers, cyclists parade through Bowness, Windermere, and show off their machines. A bicycle gave a great sense of freedom, and many owners were pleased at their good fortune and took part in holiday parades and festivals.

Despite the pig and everything possibly seeming to the contrary, James Wood of Urswick, Low Furness, was a cycling demon. He was by trade a bicycle maker at Ulverston and Barrow-in-Furness. He was also fond of a bit of a lark. For a dotty bet he set out just before the First World War to cycle all the way from Liverpool to Urswick without ever once dismounting from his machine. *En route* he stopped at a roadside cottage, still on his bike, and rang the bell until a woman brought him a drink of water. Miles later he bought a pie as he leaned in at a shop doorway, then almost lost his bet as the pie slipped out of his grasp. A second pie was found for the hungry James, who made it home, never once having dismounted. How far he travelled on the pig is less certain.

A daring woman motorist of 1911. Miss Olivia Graham of Edmond Castle, Brampton, sits proudly in her American 20 hp Flanders Tourer. At the time, woman drivers locally might be counted on one hand. As she was quick to explain to anyone sufficiently and politely interested, her car has a four-cylinder engine, five brass lamps — two of them acetylene, three paraffin — and the whole thing cost £235 including extras, mainly one speedometer.

The determined Miss Graham prepared herself by having six driving lessons at the County Garage in Carlisle. Then she set out on the first of her great driving adventures. As a first trial she went to Annan and back, and discovered that it was a good idea to carry plenty of spare petrol, for she ran out while miles from home. She sent a telegram for help, and as darkness came had to beg matches from a passer-by to light up the car's lamps.

Many outings were to follow including a 700-mile (1,100km) journey to London and back; and a hair-raising holiday to John o' Groats, during which the car's transmission failed.

Essential items on Miss Graham's jaunts included a good supply of umbrellas, a tin-lined basket for provisions, hairpins, sticking plasters, bandages and a motor veil for use during the dusty dry season.

In 1914 this indomitable driver changed her Flanders for an Argyll 12/18 four-seater tourer, but though the new car, as she said nonchalantly, had thermo-syphon cooling, magneto ignition, a zenith carburetter, a multiple-disc clutch, worm drive and brakes 'acting on all four wheels simultaneously', her love for her Flanders never died. It was in her Flanders that she had tackled what she considered to be the most dangerous road in the Lake District: the Newlands Pass.

With a sister and a friend, one Miss Scott, she set out on a day trip across to the Cumbrian coast, and then turned east again and drove up into Ennerdale. The moment they sat down to picnic by Ennerdale Water, they found disconcertingly that the generous hamper lunchbasket was heavy mainly because of the ginger beer bottles and they had only a frugal supply of food. Worse, Miss Scott had but one penny in her purse and that was all the money the three women had with them. After a mistaken attempt to drive up Honister Pass — other tourists were quick to warn them about the difficulties — they turned instead to a road signposted 'To Keswick'.

'There was', said Miss Graham later, 'no indication the road was a dangerous one …'

It proved to be a one-in-five to one-in-eleven nightmare. Almost at once she was stopped by a man who begged her to give his exhausted wife a lift to the top, because even at that moment their horse-drawn coach was disappearing up a steep hill.

Miss Graham recalled: 'The lady, who was stout, looked on the point of apoplexy or heart failure and was very hot and out of breath. I took her on board …'

The Flanders went in pursuit, and eventually came up with the coach and Miss Graham let out her charge, only to find that her car was now sandwiched between a struggling horse-drawn coach in front, and a second one behind.

'Every now and again the drivers would stop to let the horses get breath. There was no room to pass, so I had to keep stopping and starting the car on this tremendously stiff ascent. The surface was rough, with here and there deep rain gutters across the road in and out of which the car lurched. The engine was consuming oil voraciously and black smoke was issuing from behind. Of course I had turned my passengers out long ago. Presently the road became a little wider, and the driver of the first coach pulled into the side and stood still for me to pass. As soon as I was far enough ahead I stopped, and quick as lightning gave the engine some more oil, and restarted again before the horses came up with me.'

Her two weary passengers eventually caught up and the three women motored down the other side of the pass.

'All this time', said Miss Graham woefully, 'we were most hungry, and on approaching Keswick poor Miss Scott was anxious to buy a bun with her penny.'

But they bypassed Keswick. They headed straight for Edmond Castle, arriving thankfully just as dinner was being served.

The road to Furness Abbey was little more than well-rolled stone and clay when this trio stopped for a little map reading. A veil was an important asset in early motoring; it not only held the hat on, it also countered the heavy dust off the roads.

An impressive line-up of motorbikes, sidecars and their proud owners at Lecks Garage, Backbarrow.

The last bit of Hardknott Pass is ahead — and probably they were wishing it wasn't. Keswick photographer G D Abraham took the photo back in 1920 and entitled it 'Stiff and Awkward', and ever since, it seems, people have been asking: did the car ever get to the top? Even today, with a modern road surface, there are still some motorists who set off up the pass and gradually wish they hadn't. The picture was used in the out-of-print *Old Lakeland Transport* and is here again to help solve a riddle.

Of course we can see that they *did* make it. The daring motorists pause near the top of Hardknott and as they look around in the wilderness there is just the thought that now they have to get back down.

A letter to the editor of the *Lakes Chronicle*, May 1907:

'Sir,

It would appear to be the general opinion that the dust, smell and danger with motors using our roads and lanes kept a great many persons away from this beautiful district last Easter, when the weather was superb and should have drawn a grand company. I believe that one or two High-Class hotels did pretty well, but the lodging keepers suffered badly.

We hear that the purchasers of hay, oats, garden stuff, etc at Kendal all ask now where it comes from, and if grown within ten yards of a road frequented by motorists they will not have it at any price. They have probably gained experience from previously buying hay from railway embankments. This was so full of smoke sulphur etc that it gave the horses ulcerated stomachs and is no longer sold, but burnt on the spot.

Our beautiful roads are having their face entirely ruined by the sucking action of rubber tyres on motor cars, and the cost of repairing the roads all falls on the rates.

It would be well if Wealthy Motorists would avoid the roads of the Lake District while there are masses of pedestrians about, as on bank holidays, Easter, Whit week, or the local or Grasmere sports.

Some of the motor cars driven by butchers, bakers, etc might be stopped by the police at such times.

It has been said that in some parts when motors had demonstrated that they were a nuisance, loose macadam, or road metal, as it is called, was put down at quarter-mile intervals across the road, which induced the motorists to try some other route.

The authorities might very well protect the interests of this district by pursuing a similar course.

A RATEPAYER'

Ulverston coach owner Edgar Hadwin peers out from the wheel of one of his buses, one he rebuilt from the parts of several others. The party is about to set out on an outing and if Edgar's expression, and that of some of his passengers, seems a bit grim, it may be because an artist's brush at some unknown time appears to have been hard at work heavily retouching the picture. Out of his enterprising pioneering days, Edgar built up and ran a highly successful modern coach company.

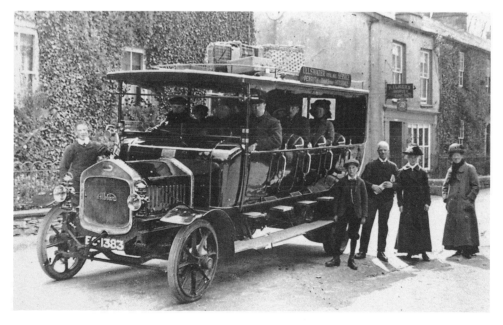

The gleaming Ullswater Royal Mail motor coach pauses at Patterdale on one of its twice-daily journeys to Penrith and back, 1915. Solid tyres, plenty of fresh air and loads of space atop for luggage.

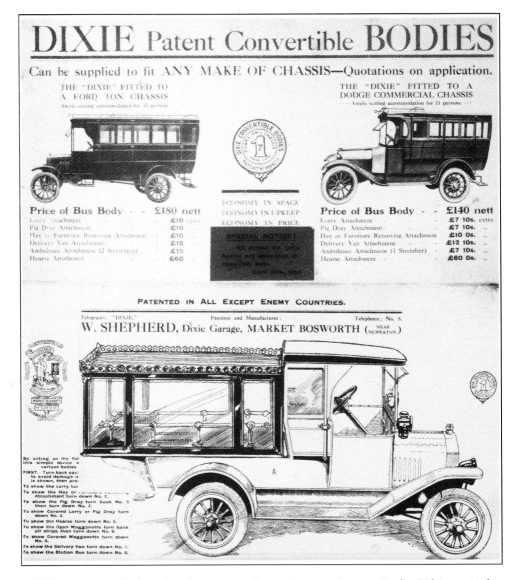

Vehicles are not always what they seem. One advert read menacingly: 'This car is the death sentence of the horse for light work'. And another: 'The pig's first and last bus ride — *to market*'.

The Dixie was owned by the Mandale family at Greystoke. Each week as a bus it carried farmers' wives and villagers into Penrith or Carlisle to do their shopping. And not only people, but baskets of butter went with them, and eggs, and crates of hens all for sale in the markets. That was one use for the Dixie. But there were others, for it was a super convertible vehicle, and was frequently rejigged and used as a coal lorry, a wagonette, a delivery van, an ambulance and even, on sombre occasions, as a hearse. Conversion took about fifteen minutes.

Some early buses were so grand that you simply had to stop and take a look. Passengers had inside accommodation, though the drivers were less well off. This solid-tyred chugger with its hefty levers drew up in King Street in Penrith and soon had admirers.

People are surprised occasionally when they hear that Britain's first airship was built in the county we now call Cumbria. And that the country's first waterplanes took off from Windermere. While a lake seems a suitable place for the latter, it might just as easily have been on a loch. The stories behind these ventures often reveal considerable determination by their promoters.

One indirectly involved was Bowness photographer Frank Herbert, a lively old man when I knew him, and rich in stories of the early flying days when he literally hung out of the cockpit of a string, canvas and bamboo-strutted plane with a half-plate camera and took photos of the lake sliding past at 45mph (70kmh). The photograph above shows Bowness as seen from the air in July 1912. Tables are set out on the lawn for tea at the Old England Hotel, while behind is St Martin's Church. To the right of the church is a white oblong patch, the skylight of the Herbert family's photographic studio where the original of this picture was processed.

He showed me a raincoat covered in stains, a souvenir from the time that one of the waterplanes, the *Waterhen*, set off from the shore of Windermere. On that occasion Frank was on shore with others, grimly holding on to the plane's tail to help the engine develop enough thrust before they let go. For their trouble, as it took off the helpers were sprayed with castor oil, with which the engine was lubricated.

'My missis played hell! — and by the way, don't go calling them seaplanes. They were *waterplanes*. Or hydroplanes, if you want.'

This was First World War material, the war to end all wars. Seaplanes did come of course, and they too flew in trials up and down Windermere.

The drone of an engine reverberates overhead as a waterplane, the *Waterhen*, flies across Bowness Bay, Windermere. Flimsy looking, and built with bamboo struts, it hardly suggests a story of success, yet that it what it was.

From the start the plane makers had set themselves a hard task, to build an aircraft capable of lifting off the water under its own power. Many people were convinced that it was impossible, though a few were intent on trying. Over at Silver Holme, on Windermere's western side, Oscar Gnosspelius, an enterprising civil engineer, was busy designing one such waterplane, helped by Arthur Borwick of the Bowness Bay yacht-building firm. A second contender was Captain Edward Wakefield, a Kendal manufacturer. And at Barrow-in-Furness a group of enthusiastic members of the Royal Navy likewise were hoping to be the first to achieve lift-off. It was not exactly a public race, but it *was* a race of a kind.

In 1910, as aircraft engines grew more reliable and the spectacle of air displays gripped the public, Gnosspelius hurried to build his plane. The problems he faced were many, particularly the design of the float. He tried variation after variation, but success always just seemed to elude him.

At Barrow-in-Furness, Cdr Oliver Schwann of the Royal Navy, in the privately formed Hermone Flying Club, took off from Cavendish dock in an Avro D on the 18th November 1911. His hopes were high, yet all too quickly they were shattered. For some fifty to sixty yards (45-55m) he flew in a kind of skipping flight, then unexpectedly, to the dismay of all involved, the plane leapt fifteen to twenty feet (4.5-6m), and collapsed into the water.

Back on Windermere, Captain Wakefield's aircraft, the *Waterbird*, now faced the challenge. This Avro Curtiss-type biplane was the forerunner of the *Waterhen* seen in

The *Waterhen* is rowed back to base. The biplane demanded real flying skills, for it was capable of plunges of fifty feet (45m) or more if it hit an air pocket. Even so, primitive looking though it is, it gave good service.

the pictures on the previous two pages. The *Waterbird* was built for the captain by A V Roe and Company of Manchester. It had a 50hp Gnome engine, with floats by Borwicks. Wakefield engaged Henry Stanley Adams, a quiet, able man, to be the test pilot. On the 25th November 1911, Adams was ready to try out the *Waterbird*. Early in the day he set out from Wakefield's property at the Hill of Oaks.

Windermere was calm as he opened up the engine, and his chances seemed good, but all did not go well. Dismayingly, the *Waterbird* failed to lift off and Adams taxied back disappointed. Then a gentle wind began to blow and Adams decided to try again. Once more he opened the engine to the full. He taxied towards the distant ferry, built up his speed, and suddenly the plane lifted clear. It rose to about fifty feet (45m), heading towards Cockshot Point just south of Belle Isle, turned and flew back. Excited cheers greeted Adams as he landed safely on the lake at the Hill of Oaks.

The *Waterbird* was succeeded by the *Waterhen*, a two-seater, again owned by Wakefield. This proved to be one of the most reliable waterplanes of its time, flying from 1912 to well into 1916. From this plane photographer Frank Herbert, of the Herbert studio in Bowness, took the earliest aerial views of Windermere, and in the exciting times that lay ahead was to photograph many memorable pictures of Windermere's waterplanes.

Early in these pioneer days, Wakefield formed his Lakes Flying Company and Adams was made a partner. Hangars were built at the Hill of Oaks, and the company set about the serious business of building planes and training pilots. This venture lasted until 1914 and the coming of the war, when Adams volunteered for active service. Wakefield sold his flying school to the Northern Aircraft Company, of Newcastle-upon-Tyne, and strings of trainee pilots began to flow through. Typical fees for training in 1915 were £75 the course, with lesser sums for military or naval officers. The company might have gone on for a long time but the Admiralty, concerned at friction at the school between civilians and military staff, took over in 1916, and the pilots and trainees were absorbed into the forces.

Not everyone approved of these pioneer flights. In 1911, prompted by a letter of complaint that an aviator – it was Captain Wakefield — was applying to put up an alleged unsympathetic hangar on the shore of the lake, that fiery countryside champion, Canon Hardwicke Rawnsley, looked into the matter. Within weeks a gale of resistance blew up. Angry letters appeared in newspapers. Ten thousand people eventually signed a protest petition which was taken to Parliament. As a result, the district council felt obliged to impose some restrictions.

The author Beatrix Potter was among the protestors. She feared that the planes would frighten the stagecoach horses on Windermere ferry and cause them to bolt, and she had a point. There were plenty of opportunities for scary moments. In August 1916, for example, the waterplanes made 142 flights on 27 days of the month, several of them too low and too close to the old ferry for comfort.

The training flights went on until August 1917. Then RNAS Windermere was closed by the Admiralty. A change of policy had been ordered by the Air Training Department at Cranwell.

Dark against the Lakeland sky, the Gnosspelius Number 2 monoplane drones over Windermere, successfully airborne, though too late to be the first plane in Britain to achieve lift-off and true flight off the water. The man behind the plane, the often-overlooked Oscar Gnosspelius, deserves our admiration — he certainly has mine — for his determination and pluck.

The civil engineer, of Swedish descent, lived at Silver Holme, Graythwaite, Windermere, and was in the forefront of the attempts to design a successful British hydroplane. Oscar's work on the pioneering aircraft, the Number 1, was already well advanced by the time Captain Edward Wakefield at Hill of Oaks got fully into the picture.

Many problems faced these early aviation addicts. Among them in particular for Oscar was finding the correct power-to-weight ratio to overcome the resistance of the floats; and of course the design of the floats themselves. He made frequent modifications, without success, and to his great disappointment, his first monoplane failed to achieve lift-off.

Nor did the prospects of the Gnosspelius Number 2 seem any better, for there were numerous setbacks. Not until the 13th February 1912 did Oscar truly get the Number 2 airborne. His monoplane achieved a series of straight 150-yard (135m) flights, on each occasion the plane rising to five feet (1.5m) or so. Later, out of this modest start grew real flight success and the Number 2 was constantly in the sky over Windermere. By then, though, Wakefield across the lake had already won the race to achieve lift-off from water.

Airpower on the slipways at the Hill of Oaks Windermere.

The engine roars as a Short aircraft is tuned at the Hill of Oaks, Windermere. The plane was built by the Fairey Aviation Company. Initially magneto troubles beset a number of the aircraft, though not apparently the 827 8560, which this is said to be. The plane undertook its acceptance flights in December 1916, and eventually was sent by rail to the school of gunnery at Loch Doon, Ayrshire, where among its many tasks it was used for instructional flights.

Before the crash … aviator Gustav Hamel, in a raincoat, stands apprehensively in front of his Blériot, listening to the organisers at Workington Sports as he tries to make up his mind whether the winds are too strong for him to risk a flight. The crowd waits to see if he will.

Workington Sports Committee decided that a daring flying display would help to attract people to their 1913 sports day. Three flights by a Blériot aircraft were advertised for the 23rd August, with a special treat as an inducement — a passenger would be carried each time, *free*. That was the promise.

Spectators poured into Lonsdale Park, where aviator Hamel was gloomily eyeing a worsening sky. In April he had been the first aviator to fly non-stop between England and Germany. Now his skills were about to be put to another test, whether to face the obviously developing gale, or whether to cancel the flight and face the anger of the crowd.

He chose the gale. Judiciously he decided to take his mechanic up with him as a passenger, seeing this as less of a risk with the locals should anything go wrong. Bravely, if perhaps foolhardily, they took off into the driving gale. The plane climbed to 1,000 feet (330m) and it headed round the iron and the steel works. In boisterous headwinds they returned to the park, and on arrival Hamel was dismayed to see that spectators were pouring across the landing zone. Desperately he turned to look for another suitable place. He rejected the shingly beach and then, seeing nothing better, to the crowd's surprise, he ditched the Blériot in rough water at the edge of the sea. The two men waded ashore to safety as people rushed down to help rescue the plane.

Fourteen thousand were there to see it all happen. The sports committee's comments were not to hand. Hamel's likewise would probably be interesting.

Enticingly the *Daily Mail* offered a small fortune, a prize of £10,000 — and all that the contestants had to do was to fly 1,010 miles (1,620km) round Britain. But it was still only 1911, and the aircraft of that pioneering period were frequently stranger than fiction and prone at times to come down unexpectedly rather than stay up. Twenty-two aviators entered the Circuit of Britain Air Race, and Carlisle had a particular interest for it was chosen as one of the staging posts.

The contestants came from Britain and abroad, and among the leading pilots was a man already known in the city, Samuel Franklin Cody. People still remembered 1899 when the showman visited Carlisle with his play *The Klondyke Nugget*. Now, in the year of 1911, he was competitor number twenty, preparing with the rest to fly from Brooklands in Surrey to Stirling and back. The race would start on the 22nd July and the first aviator was expected at the Swifts in Carlisle on the 25th. More than 25,000 people gathered to watch. But would Cody arrive first? There was plenty of speculation.

At 11.15am shouts sounded as a plane wavered into sight. But it was not Cody, it was a Blériot flown by Frenchman Andre Beaumont. Amid great excitement it made a perfect touchdown. Beaumont, exhausted, retreated rapidly to the safety of an hotel to rest. Thirty minutes later a second plane appeared, a Morane-Borel, flown by another Frenchman, Jules Vedrines. This time it was not just exhaustion — the pilot

Samuel Cody prepares for take-off at Carlisle in 1911, and his departure nearly turned into a disaster. Excited helpers are said to have held on to one of the wings a bit too long and dismayingly the plane veered towards the River Eden. Cody struggled with the controls and managed to lift clear, turning his plane and flying off through a lucky gap in the trees.

was unwell and had to lie down on the grass to try to overcome air sickness. News of Vedrines' arrival reached Beaumont who decided too much was at stake and, not wanting to waste any more time, he hurried back to his machine and set off again on the next leg, 103 miles (165km) to the Manchester control.

Next day at Carlisle, James Valentine arrived in a Deperdussin monoplane. Trouble awaited him, too. Strong winds were proving troublesome and he suffered a whole day's frustrating delay waiting for them to abate.

In all this, where was Cody? Word came at last that he had left Paisley. The crowds, much reduced, waited and were surprised when Cody arrived, not in a plane, but in a horse-drawn cab. He explained that he had had to land at Lanark and had caught an express train to ask Carlisle to keep the control open for just one more day. Which Carlisle obligingly did. He flew his biplane in the next day, the first all-British entry to arrive. That evening Cody even managed a late stop-over lecture at Her Majesty's Theatre about his aerial adventures, a useful fill-in while his plane's engine was urgently de-coked.

Between 2,000 to 3,000 spectators were at the Swifts at 4am the next morning when he took off again. He decided to take the west coast route and flew to the Solway Firth, then inland where he followed the railway to Maryport. Windy conditions proved to be a problem and cautiously he landed briefly in a field near Workington's Ellerbeck Hospital, and again in a field at Moresby where he had breakfast, followed by a shave in a Whitehaven barber's. He resumed his flight later in the day, after being delayed by the blustery wind.

The popular Cody did not win the race — Beaumont scored there — but in the end he did finish, and he received a modest cash award. And had managed a shave.

The Lad Could Do Everything

THE HIRING OF farmhands and servants was the oldest form of labour exchange known, possibly six centuries or even more. But it could be a withering experience. Youngsters might stand all morning in a street while farmers and their wives looked them over, much as they might examine a cow or a horse at a sale ring, and then they would bargain about their wages. It happened each Whitsuntide, and at each Martinmas in November.

'Is tha for hire, lad?'

'Aye, master.'

A Cumbrian boy of fourteen, fresh from home and wanting to earn his living, showed so like others around him by setting a piece of straw in the corner of his mouth, or a match in his cap, or sometimes showing a small artificial posy in his jacket lapel.

'And what can you do, then?'

Could he hoe, scale muck, plough, stitch a furrow, mow, handle a harrow, repair a wall? Well, the bolder lad could do it all. And there was a chant:

> 'Can thou plough and muck and harrow, boy?
> Can thou shovel shit, and wheel a barrow, boy?'

And again the lad could. So the farmer would find out if the boy had worked elsewhere already, or if anyone knew him, and he might arrange to meet the boy again later in the morning after getting his *character*. It was a gamble on both sides. With this in mind, in 1909 in Kendal the farmers even started a voluntary system of character books, but the experiment did not last.

One of the oldest hiring jokes tells of a youth who agreed to work for a farmer, but the man decided to find out about the boy first. They met again an hour later.

'Well, I's getting thee character', said the farmer, nodding agreeably. 'And it's all right, me lad. You can start Monday.'

'Aye', says the youth. 'And I's getting' thine, and I's not coming.'

Pay was another important matter.

'And how much is tha asking?'

'Six pounds, master.'

'Nay!' The farmer would shake his head, his face blank. 'I's not wanting to hire *two* on you. How would five pounds do?'

And so the bargaining would begin. Eventually the pay would be agreed, usually a compromise. Thus a farmer's wife to a girl who had asked for £5 for the half-year: 'Can you be milking?' And if the girl shook her head: 'Then how if I give thee four pounds ten shillings, and I learn you to milk?' The girl would agree to start a week later and stay the full six months.

Typical bargains struck in Ulverston in 1906 at the Whit Thursday hiring fair, all including board and lodgings, were £20 for a head man for the half-year; boys and youths, £5 to £12; dairy maids to £15; women, £11 to £13; second-class women (whatever that might mean) £8 to £10; girls, £5 to £7. The hiring term was twenty-four to twenty-six weeks, including a holiday week at the end of each term. To clinch the hiring, the farmer would give the hired man or woman a sixpence or a shilling, known variously as a *yearl*, *earl*, *arle* or *earnest money*. It was a recognised token of the half-year's service to come, and usually ended being spent there and then at the hiring fair, often enough on beer.

In later times, wages rose little by little; some years, better bargains could be struck by the hired, especially if there were a labour shortage; some years, if the weather were favourable and crops were well advanced, the farmers had the edge. Both sides were quick to appreciate where any advantage lay.

Not all hired servants turned up for work. Some risked prison, kept the shilling (it rose to half a crown (12^1/$_2$p) in later times), and went on to other hirings and tried for a better bargain with another farmer. Some did the rounds, accepting several yearls, before vanishing. Contemporary newspapers tell of a few who were caught and gaoled. But the danger of being found seems to have been minimal. The hirings saw large numbers of men and women on the move, and pursuing runaways was usually too time-consuming to follow through. Farmers remembered, though, and sometimes the guilty were encountered at later hirings.

While many farmers were good employers, some quite definitely were not. Farms where they were mean with food, particularly with meat, were widely known as 'bad tommy (tummy) spots'. Reputations travelled swiftly among the hired crowds. It is occasionally told of a farm where the hired men were surprised to learn by chance that there was going to be *real* stew for dinner that day, meat having been a rarity. They were suitably surprised, for meat it turned out to be, but, full of *mowks* (maggots), though all, as they were informed, 'well cooked'.

However, while the sharper unpleasant memories are usually the ones that survive, and while hired hands could tell of poor workplaces, it was also the case that many landed on agreeable farms and remained happily for years.

'Will you be thinking to stay on, then, John?' The question usually arose as each hiring time neared. And a typical answer might be: 'Aye, master, if you can see your way to a bit more pay.'

Some hired men and women servants in time have been treated as members of the family, benefiting in wills, occasionally even being left land. Two brothers I met on a small farm near Ulverston in Furness were in fact a widowed farmer and his hired man, sitting in old age by their fireside, grown to look alike, sharing the place that both had worked down the years. Another time, to our own door came a former labourer who had been left an entire farm where he had worked, a short distance from Keswick, and who had gone on to buy two more and became a millionaire. Exceptions, of course, but it happened occasionally.

In general, farmers and ambitious labourers approved of the system of hiring. The masters knew that a well-fed single man who lived in would work long hours without trouble and for a while would be highly productive. And a hardworking, thrifty hired man who saved his earnings, and perhaps married an equally thrifty woman, could hope to rent and eventually perhaps own his own farm. Way back, there are interesting savings recorded for farm labourers. The 1868 report of Penrith's branch of the Carlisle Savings Bank, for example, showed the amount due to 260 men farm servants totalled more than £9,259; and to 240 women farm servants, £7,904 — not, of course, all saved in a single year.

On the down side, the system has been compared to a slave market. Women in particular disliked having to stand in the street and be scrutinised as if they were cattle. The waiting ordeal might last an hour, or even two, during a typical hiring morning, with many men and women stopping to question the waiting girls. Seizing on this, servants' agencies opened up in shops and church halls, and in this way many women were placed in service more discreetly. Thus at Kendal, concerned local women in 1895 booked a hall for female hiring and it proved a popular system. Likewise, at Penrith, where St Andrew's Parish rooms were open as a free registry for servant women and employers, from nine o'clock to one, with refreshments at a small cost. Otherwise, many women were hired on the recommendation of friends, and often that proved the best way.

Councils sometimes tried to organise the hirings and improve their image. In Lowther Street, Carlisle, signs were put up in among the crowd labelled 'Boys' and 'Girls' to show where they must stand. The attempts seem to have met with little success. An old-timer once quoted me a few of the hands' comments, but they were a little too vivid for here.

The social disadvantages of the hiring system included illegitimacy. While illegitimacy in Edwardian England was on the decline, farm workers might change their masters many times, and a man who had got a farm girl pregnant could simply vanish at the next hiring into the crowd to a new job. Masters, too, did not always enjoy the best of reputations in this respect. Mothers of young girls were well aware of the risks. Hence the view that agencies were the best way for a young girl to find work, suitably supervised by their mother or a sister. Local shop owners, as in Ulverston and elsewhere, while selling toys and such, also advertised themselves as servants' agencies.

Hirings were held in many towns including Appleby, Carlisle, Penrith, Kendal. Wigton, Workington, Whitehaven and down at Bootle, Ulverston and

Barrow-in-Furness. Men who failed to secure a job at Carlisle on a Saturday, perhaps holding out for better pay, would walk on to Monday's hiring at Cockermouth. And those who still failed to get work had another chance at the second hirings, usually a week later in some towns.

It is hard to say when the last Cumbrian hiring took place, though as late as 1953 a few labourers turned up on Whitsun Saturday at Carlisle Cross and struck their bargains, but it was a pale reminder of the great crowds of the past.

Situations Vacant & Wanted

WANTED, at Whitsuntide, a tidy, respectable GIRL, about 16.—Apply, Mrs. CROSBY, Prospect House, Kirkbythore.

WANTED, at the term, a good, strong GIRL for farm house, one able to milk.—Apply to T. JACKSON, Thwaite Hall, Greystoke, Penrith.

WANTED, a MORNING GIRL.—Apply, MITRE INN, Penrith.

WANTED, at the term, a strong GIRL, about 16.—Apply, Mrs. THOMPSON, Confectioner, Devonshire-street, Penrith.

WANTED, at the term, a good, strong GIRL. —Apply, WILLIAMSGILL, Templesowerby.

WANTED, a Country GIRL for the Kitchen, about 16; another kept.—Apply to Mrs. IRVING, 13, Lowther-street, Penrith.

WANTED, at Whitsuntide, a GIRL for a farm house, able to milk.—Apply, H. JACKSON, Rose Bank, Templesowerby.

WANTED, now or at Whitsuntide, a NURSE GIRL.—Apply to Mrs. HARRINGTON, Long Ashes, Penrith.

Mid-Cumberland and North Westmorland Herald, May 7, 1904

Organising the hirings. The city council tries to bring order to the milling throng in Lowther Street, Carlisle. Boards labelled 'Boys' and 'Girls' are being tried, but attempts to show the young labouring class where to stand met with little success.

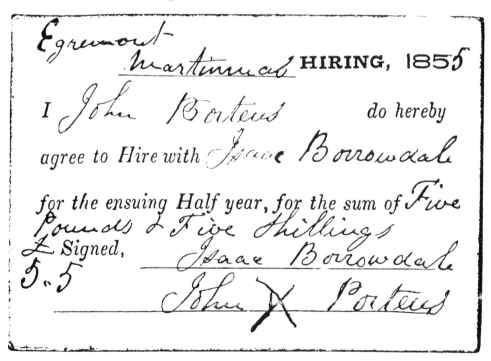

A hiring receipt. John Porteus has made his mark at the Martinmas hirings in Egremont and agrees to work for Isaac Borrowdale for the next half-year.

The lad could do everything . . . Farmer's boy, ten-year-old Tom Bryson proves the point and plays the horses a tune on his concertina. It's 1919 and young Tom lived at Housenrigg Farm, Langrigg, Aspatria. He became a lorry driver later in life driving everything from taxies to buses and petrol tankers, delivering fuel to airfields during the 1939-45 war. He kept his love of music, playing in a lively group, The Four Bs.

Annie Threlkeld tells of how she was hired in her home town of Penrith in 1906 as a farm lass …

Well, I went and stood on a street, and the bosses and mistresses did likewise. I was walking slowly along when a horrible scruffy looking man came along and said: 'Are you to hire?' I didn't speak, and kept on walking and a woman stopped and said: 'Are you engaged?'

Well she seemed all right, and I said no. So she started talking, asking how much I wanted. I said £10 for the half-year and she said could I milk? I said no, so she said: 'I'll give you nine, and learn you to milk'. And she gave me a shilling as earls money.

I stayed there two years. They were nice folk and looked after you; I was only allowed out on Sunday after I'd finished work, and that was in time for church at 6.30pm. And had to be back at 9pm. If I were a few minutes late she was at the gate waiting for you with a watch.

You were kept at it all day, from 5am, but it did us no harm.

Every Time She Coughs

After the morning hirings, it was time for the fairs — often fun, and sometimes not. Each Whitsuntide and Martinmas saw a cavalcade of showmen and their caravans coming down out of Scotland or arriving from many parts of England to set up their stands and stalls in the Cumbrian towns.

For the showmen it was often a big social event, a time to meet old friends and exchange adventures. And for the newly hired young men and women, the fairs were a chance to let off steam and be rid of any frustration. The crowds poured in, and with them moved the pedlars, the quack doctors and the pickpockets. Drunkenness was rife and the danger of a farm labourer's six months' earnings vanishing in the fun was real enough. But there was plenty to see and enjoy and, for the more careful, there was always a chance you might meet a future spouse.

At Penrith, after the hirings in Sandgate, also held in Burrowgate, the fair and merry making took place in Great Dockray. At Carlisle the fair was at the Sands. In Cockermouth an amazing conglomeration of stalls and sideshows engulfed Main Street. Similar scenes took place in other market towns.

And there was plenty to go at: hobby horses, hooplas, old Aunt Sally, donkey rides, swingboats, a multitude of stalls; the pig with six feet, a calf with two heads; shooting galleries, fortune tellers, boxing booths and much more.

The fat lady attracted a big crowd. Annie Parker, who lived near the old maternity hospital in Carlisle, recalled one particular spieler. 'Really rude, he was! A really grubby face. "Come and see the fat lady!" he yelled. "Every time she coughs she wees!" Well, as you can guess, the men always gathered round that one!'

Lottie Brough, who was hired at Penrith and worked just a few miles from Keswick, loved the fairs. She too remembered the fat lady:

'The fat lady, I remember she come out of her booth and let us see how fat she is; held up her leg with her skirt up. She invited us folk to have a look. The spieler calls out: "Come on, lads, she'll let you feel her leg. It's all reet. Come on now! The fattest lady on earth. Would you like to feel her leg?" One lad come up and felt her, said: 'By God, that's a good leg." Well a lot laughed at that! She was fat all reet.

'One time there was an animal thing in a cage. Like a monkey, but big. You got to push it with a stick for a ha'penny and it made a noise like a fart. Some pushed it a lot of times and didn't get no fart, and the spieler got one on the nose for cheating. Didn't like it myself. The fat lady was better.'

Boxing booths were immensely popular. Burly farm lads eyed up the wiry-looking boxers and, often half-drunk, needed little encouragement from their friends to join the queue in the hope of winning an easy cash prize. Once inside the ring, the pugilist let the farmhand gain a few advantages in the opening rounds, and then he set about finishing him off. Occasional the pro was surprised and himself took a beating, but in general the dice were loaded. Referees and the seconds were on the side of the boxer, and if he did get into trouble the bell had a way of sounding early. Really tough-looking farm lads were often given training gloves to wear, big things that were strapped high up the arms and ponderously heavy. Against the light fighting gloves of the pro, the farm lads rarely won. One Carlisle boxer I knew in Denton Holme had never once lost to a farm lad, and he had fought hundreds.

If boxing booths were a great source of enjoyment, so too were the fortune tellers, the shrewd-eyed gypsies. Women would queue to have their fortunes told, and evidently they were given satisfaction because they came out of the booths laughing and comparing notes.

Alehouses likewise were crowded. It was a great time for dancing. Most public houses had a fiddle player and an accordionist or pianist and a room for dancing. Fights erupted frequently as the ale took hold and one man or another tried to poach another's girl, and each time it happened the more experienced bands would retreat swiftly to safety until it was quiet enough to resume playing. At the end of a busy fair day it could be risky simply to push through the crowds. Contemporary newspapers record instances of innocent passers-by being clobbered as drunken bodies were pitched out of alehouses and landed in among them.

Roundabouts and sideshows crowd along Cockermouth's Main Street at the centuries-old fair. The noisy fairs followed on the Whitsuntide and Martinmas morning hirings, which at their peak attracted into the town around a thousand prospective farmworkers. Sometimes the hiring advantage was to the hired, but in the acute depression of the 1930s, the flood of candidates for hire swelled and farmers reaped a rich harvest of ultra-cheap labour. This busy scene was before the traffic grew too difficult and the local council banished the fair to the town's Fairfield car park.

Hard-hatted showmen stand up on the platforms fronting the ornate fair booths on the Sands at Carlisle as they set about enticing the crowd to step inside and see the shows. Looming behind is the Turf Hotel. From the grandstand on the roof, horse racing on the nearby Swifts course could be watched.

A crowd of men and women flows along the lines of show booths and stalls at Kendal. The hirings are over for another six months and the fair is in full swing.

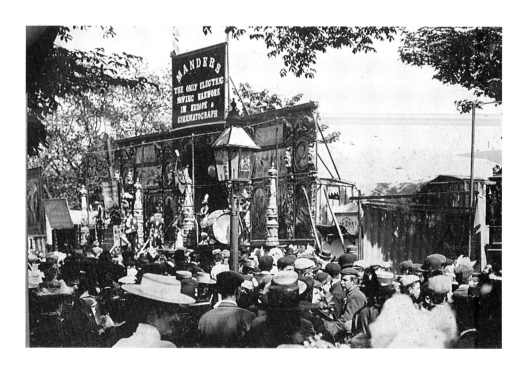

Opposite:
Fashionably dressed women and children pause at a merry-go-round at Kendal hiring fair. Fairground shows often travelled considerable distances. Many, including Manders Waxworks and others, moved from hiring fair to hiring fair, beginning business after the morning hirings had taken place. Some stayed the one day, before packing everything up and moving on to the next venue, sometimes travelling through the night.

Ice cream time at a Carlisle hirings fair. Often the fair had some new attraction. At the horse tent the spieler worked hard: 'Roll up! Roll up! The strangest thing that ever you'll see, a horse's *head*, where it's *tail* should be!' In people went, and came out grinning. 'Nay, it's right enough!' Others followed to find a stall with a horse standing there — its tail towards the manger, and its head facing the visitors.

Opposite, below:
Enterprisingly one of the booths at Kendal hiring fair is showing film allegedly from the Transvaal War, but all may not be as it seems. Scenes of troops engaged in battle in South Africa were sometimes faked in London film studios, a practice that caused a scandal. Manders was a popular fairground show with its claim to be 'The only electric moving waxworks in Europe & cinematograph.'

While hiring fairs were once a vigorous part of Cumbrian life, other fairs took place which had a different emphasis, as at Kirkby Stephen. Here horse trading is in full swing at the annual Cowper Day fair. Men on horseback clop along the cobbles under the eye of would-be buyers, goods are unloaded at a shop, men stand round the carts, and an excited group of bareback ponies nuzzles together as the crowd examines their worth.

Cowper Day fair, *cowper* possibly meaning Gill Fair, took place in September. The horses — and ponies, brought into town straight off the fells — used to be sold in the streets themselves. To a sudden clatter of hooves, the sellers would come running through the crowd of would-be buyers, their horses in tow, showing off their paces. It was an exciting, noisy event, with hard bargaining, each sale concluding with the traditional slap of the hand between seller and buyer.

The Elephants are Coming

SUDDENLY THE CIRCUS is expected, and especially the elephants. The town centre seems to be full of activity. Flotillas of children are dashing about, and people are waiting and talking. Annual visits by travelling circuses seemed to bring out the entire population. As the elephants plod into sight, the excited children trail the procession, weaving through the crowd, getting up alongside the wagons and animals, and being shooed away for their trouble. A circus visit might often be the entertainment highlight of the year. In remoter areas, where the circus would simply rumble through, it was treat enough for many an excited youngster just to see the ornate wagons going past.

If you wanted a cool splash on a hot summer's day, where better than in Bowness Bay, Windermere, especially if you were an elephant. Travelling circuses put on their performances up the hill at Goodly Dale field. Watching the elephants squirt water was a hugely popular pastime, though over-curious visitors sometimes found themselves taking part in the cooling process. Likewise, local children. Numerous youngsters have arrived home to spankings for turning up drenched.

The elephants and camels plod into town, and one can only wonder how far they have come and how weary they might be. Despite the dreariness of the street, there was always magic in the air when a travelling circus and its menagerie arrived, and soon the crowd begins to gather.

Tall hat, long legs: a clown steps out boldly on stilts. The picture, from West Cumbria, is from the 1890s. Local lads, many in knickerbockers and clogs, trail the swaying figure as he moves through town, advertising the next circus performance.

Sturdy teams of fine greys clatter into Wigton, watched by a crowd of bystanders. Two towering floats are in tow, crowned by the performers and their bands. It was a fine sight, and greatly anticipated by town and country folk alike.

When Labour was Cheap

For many Cumbrians more than a century ago, the working week lasted for fifty-five hours or more. Conditions were often poor and work was often strenuous. Throughout England labour was cheap, with domestic service the largest single occupation. This last helped to drain away many young Cumbrians from the rural areas to the towns, girls especially. It was cheaper for middle-class families to engage maids than to buy labour-saving equipment.

Work was often scarce and at times men fought for jobs. For many, if a family were to stay above the poverty line, it required constant work. Women, at times in desperation, set off to cross the country itself to find jobs, even if sometimes it meant earning less than a living wage.

A woodcutter's hut near Keswick. The structure, built a bit like a wigwam, is covered with overlapping sods. While similar in shape to those used by charcoal burners, the one here may have been used by bark peelers, for it appears to have a characteristic stone-built hearth which extends externally from the walls. Such cabins were occupied longer than those used by the charcoal colliers, and sometimes the men's families turned up to join them — in this instance with a generous tablecloth — and stayed for a few days. The stripped bark was sold to the tanneries.

Men living on the edge of danger: the Lowwood gunpowder workers at Haverthwaite, c1890. Seven gunpowder work sites existed in Lakeland, with Lowwood, built in 1799, on the River Leven. Together they supplied the country with most of its gunpowder. Copper and lead mining and slate quarrying were among its Cumbrian uses, but nationally it was also exported to West Africa, where it was used in the exchange of slaves.

Six Lowwood workers were killed in an explosion in 1863, the blast so loud it was heard some thirteen miles (21 km) away at Kendal. Five more were killed five years after that, and others died in 1887 and 1903. Women also worked at Lowwood, packing cartridges. During thunderstorms, as a precaution they fled to the shelter of safer, more distant buildings.

The other gunpowder works included Blackbeck at nearby Bouth. It had a bad reputation for accidents, and between 1867 and 1911 twenty-seven people died.

The danger from sparks was always present. Protective measures varied from works to works but included over-shoes, pocketless clothing to help eliminate metal objects, copper hooves for horses, and non-ferrous rails, as on the tramways between Lowwood and Blackbeck.

Demand for the Black Powder, as it was often called, decreased after the First World War. One by one the works closed, Lowwood in 1934, and Gatebeck, south-east of Kendal, in 1937.

A field worker and helpers. John Stalker shows off his glittering nailed boots, while his sons keep to good old clogs. It's a pause during haytiming at Howhead Farm, overlooking Coniston Water, c1890. Rain was one of the main enemies.

Haytiming often saw whole families out in the fields racing to get the crop dried and under cover, or built into stacks before the weather changed. In bad years, hay lying out blackened in rain-soaked fields is one of the dismal sights of farming.

Truancy at this time was almost an accepted part of rural life. School logs, as at Hutton Roof, Penrith, on numerous occasions record that this or that pupil was 'absent this day for haytiming.' School inspectors militantly tried to stamp out the practice, but rarely succeeded.

Charcoal burners rake through hot ash at the end of a burn near Haverthwaite. Hot bodies, blackened faces and another batch of valuable fuel near-ready.

Making charcoal was once a considerable industry, particularly in High Furness. The men were known for centuries as colliers, the term's use for coalminers being relatively recent.

The maturing wood was stockpiled ready for a burn and, when the time came, the men built up the mounds and covered them in turf, sometimes keeping several burns going at once. The coaling process could take from twenty-four hours to three or four days. Rain was the dreaded enemy. Many charcoal burners' families knew hard times if long rainy seasons prevailed.

Five tons of wood made one ton of charcoal, which was used for smelting at various ironworks, but in particular at the famous Backbarrow furnace by the River Leven, noted for its high-grade charcoal iron. For a long time charcoal was an important, effective fuel, but eventually coke was found to be more efficient.

An old woodsman, Jack Allonby of Spark Bridge, once brought me a long unbroken piece of charcoal and proudly held it out. 'Just you listen to this', he said with a grin, and he tapped the silvery-black stick with a metal bar. Astonishingly it rang almost musically. 'That's how you know it's done properly', said Jack.

When Arthur Ransome's *Swallows and Amazons* was made into a film, it was Jack who was engaged to advise during a charcoal-burning scene. Jack, in his cap and silvery whiskers, looking every bit the charcoal burner, couldn't be in the film because he wasn't a union member, but he showed the actors what to do, and agreeably they listened and made sure that everything was done properly.

Eager young faces … visiting schoolboys see how charcoal is made at a pitstead in Well Wood, Bardsea. A stack of neatly cut sticks has been built round the central stake, or *motty peg*, and awaits its cover of sods before the burn begins.

To be sold in public Sale.

At Dalegarth Hall, in the Parish of Eskdale, and County of Cumberland,

On Wednesday the 3d of December, 1806,

About sixty Acres of

OAK, ASH,

& other Coppice Wood,

OF THE GROWTH OF 17 YEARS,

Standing upon Dalegarth Hall Demesne.

Also a large Parcel of

COPPICE WOOD,

OF THE SAME DESCRIPTION,

Growing upon Kirkland Estate, in the Parish of Ponsonby, in the aforesaid County

HENRY HARTLEY will show the Wood at Dalegarth, and JOHN GUNSON that of Kirkland.

Printed by W. Pennington, Kendal.

Workmen take it easy at Gaskell's in Ulverston where a fine selection of wheels is propped against the walls. Business being business, as well as being a wheelwright, he was also a joiner and an undertaker.

Men and lads at Threlkeld granite quarry, 1890. About 150 worked there. Today Threlkeld, which is near Keswick, is a mining museum with its own steam railway.

Walking stick at the ready, the Duke of Devonshire pauses astride the rail tracks during a visit to his slate quarries at Kirkby in Furness.

Three maids pause for a cup of tea at Milnthorpe, though in reality this scene was a popular set-up with photographers. The woman on the right in spectacles is Sarah Aldren, who went into service when she was thirteen and worked fourteen hours a day. Her daughter, Mary Perry of Windermere, remembered her mother's daily work, and her own too, for she also became a maid ...

Mother's in a dress uniform: a dark dress and a white apron. Of course in the morning she wore a print dress and a plain apron while cleaning. Couldn't show her ankles. There'd have been a row with the mistress if she had. She changed her uniform ready for lunch.

If a lady or a gentleman left a card she carried it on a tray to the mistress, never in the hand. That was the rule. I don't know why. Every other Sunday she had free time to go to church to pray. Mother had to wear a bonnet when she went to church ... she was always having to change her uniforms, three times some days, depending on the time, and who called.

I got a job myself as a maid at Skelwith Bridge with a mother and a daughter. It was dreadful. The daughter had a snappy little dog and she used to speak to her dog better than to the servants. It was a beautiful house ... Oh, the old lady was a bit queer, I think I could have managed her, but the daughter I couldn't manage at all. She humiliated us. Everything was locked up. Even the candle was locked up at night after eight. It was put in a cupboard. If it all burned away, she made us buy a new one, and stopped the money out of our pay.

The old lady's husband was dead. The room where he died was 'preserved', if that's the right word. There were vases of white flowers — lilies and such, and she changed them every few days. We hadn't even to touch the bed because the mark of the coffin was still on the covers ... It were a queer spot, no mistake.

Village women in the rubbing stones factory at KirkbyThore in the Eden Valley. The stones were popular with housewives who used them to whiten floors, hearths and steps. They were made from gypsum, dug out of local quarries. It was broken up with hammers, burned in a kiln and pounded with wooden mells. Finally it was ground to powder in a mill which was powered by a circling horse. Back in this workshop, the women quickly mixed the powder with water and put it in the half-moon shaped moulds on the bench. These took ten minutes to set, then were knocked out and stacked. The air was often thick with the dust but many villagers were glad of the work. About the turn of the twentieth century at least two tonnes of gypsum were used locally each week.

There were two mills in the parish, and some 12,000 blocks went into each wagon load and were sent to the station for sale in other parts of the country.

Off to Market

THE WIVES AND the daughters churned the butter, patted it to shape, wrapped it and packed the baskets. Eggs were gathered and sorted, bread baked, jam and marmalade made, and the jars filled and labelled. Poultry was killed — or sometimes was not, but nonetheless made ready for sale, in a crate, ruffled, still clucking. Markets for many were an important part of a rural family's income.

Come the day, the cart was loaded, and off to town went the farmer and his wife. If there were no transport, women walked, a basket of produce over each arm. As an example, from Lowick, in Furness, away before dawn, five miles (8km) or so to Ulverston to set up a stall in the market square, and at day-end, all sold, time to do a bit of shopping, and then a walk home with the groceries.

Here and there were horse-drawn buses. Into Kendal, into Ulverston, into Cockermouth; Greystoke to Penrith, Thursby to Carlisle, and into other market towns. In Borrowdale, along narrow roads families climbed in for the Keswick round-trip. Horse-drawn, customarily, but then — progress — motorbuses, crates of hens jamming the luggage racks, and a mad scramble if a bird escaped down in among the passengers. It has been known.

Opposite:
The outdoor market — and time for a gossip in Keswick's market square. These well-dressed women include a sporty tennis player and a companion complete with racquet. A sign of the times is the temperance hotel, today simply the Skiddaw Hotel. Keswick's market goes back a long way, for it was a market town before 1545.

The indoor market: talk fills the hall as shoppers crowd round the stalls and tables at Carlisle's popular and spacious new covered market. The countryside has come to town, bringing fresh produce, vegetables, flowers, butter and baskets loaded with eggs.

A chair on the cobbles, with time for a quick talk, or a browse at the bookseller's stand in the Green Market, Carlisle. In the background, two locally well-known shops, Coulthards the grocers, and Bewshers the chemist and spirit dealer. And the two darkly clad women, intent, totally absorbed — whatever *were* they saying?

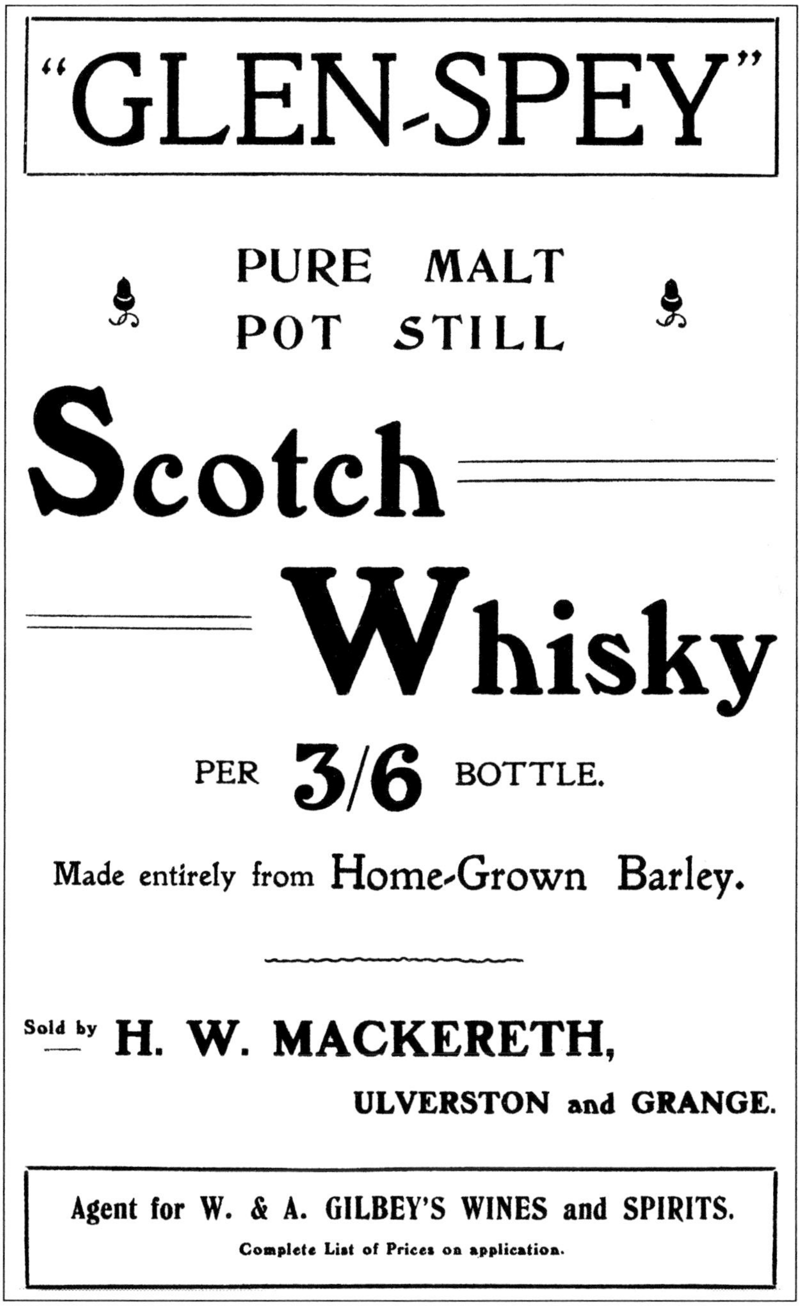

"GLEN-SPEY"

PURE   MALT
POT   STILL

Scotch ══════

══════ Whisky

PER **3/6** BOTTLE.

Made entirely from Home-Grown Barley.

Sold by **H. W. MACKERETH,**

ULVERSTON and GRANGE.

Agent for W. & A. GILBEY'S WINES and SPIRITS.

Complete List of Prices on application.

Opposite:
A sunny September day in 1914 at Penrith's busy butter market. On this occasion it was held in Sandgate when soldiers of the Westmorland and Cumberland Yeomanry slept in the market hall, which they had commandeered. This picture postcard was sent to Master W Hale at Edenhall Vicarage, Langwathby, and was signed 'Nan', who hoped he would get better soon.

Christmas surely is coming and this well-provisioned poultry shop in Workington is ready for the rush. Ducks, geese, chickens and rabbits hang with their heads down to catch the blood. It's an orderly display, the result of hours of plucking and preparation, and it's no wonder the traders look pleased.

Cairns butcher's shop in Market Square, Alston. In this shop, local lad John James Armstrong started work as a butcher's boy, delivering meat from his basket. John worked for twenty-five years for Alec Cairns, then decided to start his own shop in the town. For short spells he worked for two other butchers, Donald McKinnon and Albert Biggs, and then he risked everything and opened his own place. He was a butcher there for twenty-five more years, and it was his jest that in all the fifty years in the trade he never once managed to get a paid holiday. His starting wage in 1916 was modest enough ...

A butcher's boy, aye. It was five shilling [25p] a week when I began as an apprentice butcher. I was fourteen and Mr Cairns was the best businessman I was ever to meet.

Well, he started me off doing different little jobs, scrubbing the chopping blocks and scrubbing the floor out on Mondays, serving too, of course. And eventually I got to learning how to slaughter animals. There was no captive bolt guns, I just had to hit the beasts with a poleaxe on the forehead — had to be strong, and a good shot. The boss would chase me if I took more than one shot. Aye, I felt a bit funny at first, but got used to it.

We worked five and a half days in the shop, seven-thirty to six at night, and longer Fridays and Saturdays, sometimes eight o'clock. There were no holidays. The only days we got was Christmas and so on. Nor was there overtime. Half an hour over today and the boss would give time off in lieu tomorrow.

A lot of meat was eaten in the town. Top cuts of beef and lamb cost a shilling a pound. The cuts were never boned out; we cut it as it should be cut. All the flavour's in the bone. Meat was mature, too. Cattle were three year old before they were killed. A good flavour.

Mr Cairns bought mostly Shorthorns, at Carlisle market. And Angus. In the First World War there was little English meat — it was all from Argentina. For years the best beef came out of Argentina. Beautiful cattle.

Every Monday we bought three bullocks at Carlisle, sometimes four; and they arrived by train that night at Alston and I drove 'em up to our shed at Overburn, near our killing shed. Every butcher had his killing shed. But there was no roughing the animals about. It makes a big difference. The meat kept well because of it.

We had cold rooms. W D Marks of Carlisle called to collect the skins and hides, and he sold blocks of ice, four stone [25kg]at a time. We broke 'em up and put in a tank, layers of ice and layers of rock salt. It worked well. Like a fridge.

There was a good profit in a £20 beast. Even at a shilling a pound. Of course you could get cheaper cuts: brisket beef at threepence a pound, liver sixpence, tripe fivepence. It took a long time to prepare tripe, a couple of hours to clean it, then three more boiling it in the sett pot in the back. A five-hour business!

The job I liked best was taking the horse and trap out into the country delivering. The old butcher's trap, sitting on top. I did it for thirty years, by horse first, then in a motor van.

So on Mondays we bought cattle. Tuesdays slaughtered one of 'em and Wednesday I set off to Carrshields, over the top, eight miles [13km] or so. Be away about nine in the morning and sell to about twenty or thirty customers, at farms and cottages. The meat box was at the back; you lifted the top half and the bottom came down on a couple of chains with a chopping block. A travelling butchers.

After that it was Nenthead Thursday, Garrigill Friday, Slaggyford Saturday morning. A typical day at Garrigill might sell £10 of meat if I was lucky. Took some selling that did. The beasts just cost £20, but you'd get £40 back easily.

Winters were worst, going out in cold weather in snow and ice and bitter winds. But I never got stuck. You don't with a horse. With a motor vehicle, yes. My horse Jean knew every inch of the ground. Didn't need to say which house to stop at; she knew. She'd just stop. And she knew when she was finished, when she was coming home. Slow out, fast back. Oh yes!

But motor vehicles finished horses. Other butchers got vans so we did too. A Morris Cowley from about 1922. There and back in half the time. It's sad. But we could do two trips in a day.

My boss, Mr Cairns, he was the best judge of beef and fat sheep I've known. He stood at the ringside and put his hand on a beast and say that that was the one. Marvellous he was. Never got it wrong. He was noted for the quality of the meat he sold.

Old farmers had an odd sheep or two, fat, Blackfaced ewes. A farmer would come in the shop. 'Alec, I've got a fat ewe yonder.' He'd say: 'Just come in.' And no matter what size the ewe was, he'd say: 'Twenty-five shillin' [£1.25].' Big or little: 'Twenty-five shillin'.' He were good, he were. Real good.

On the Land

A S EDWARDIAN ENGLAND DAWNED, the new century saw many changes looming for farming. Though it was still possible for Edwardians to see fields being harvested by scythe and sickle, and cows being milked by hand, mechanisation was under way.

Large numbers of people had left the countryside, but talk of good wages awaiting in the industrial towns and cities did not always appeal, not to the older hands at least. Those who stayed did not always think working in factories and mills was better, though there was a price to pay for not trying. Agricultural wages were low. In 1907 they averaged I7s 6d (87½p) a week nationally. And farming was changing. A village like Stainton, near Penrith, which had 17 farms in 1901 had only six in 1985. Amalgamations of course played their part.

In the old Lakeland counties of Cumberland, Westmorland and North Lancashire, growing food a century ago was harder in many ways than now. Ploughing needed the skill to manage two or three horses, as well as a lot of stamina. Just to plough a single acre (0.4ha) in nine-inch (23cm) furrows with a pair of heavy horses could mean a walk of twelve to thirteen miles (19-21km). A good man would do about an acre a day, depending how hard the going, but also how strong and well he might feel. Just as important, his rate of progress depended on how strong and how well his horse might be.

Some jobs could be a real misery, among them thinning turnips and weeding. Groups of men and women, sometimes even children, crawled on their hands and knees for miles from field end to field end, pulling out the weeds, thinning the plants. The task was eased by tying sacking or canvas round their legs, but rheumatism was a price that many paid.

Women were often used as cheap labour for the hardest of field jobs, including muck spreading, gathering potatoes and — one of the most barren of all crops — the picking of stones off the land. At times, whole families spent days out in the fields doing just that, picking up the stones in their thousands, clearing them away. Even now, in this desperate new millennium, there is a family a few miles from my home which sets aside a day each year to go into the fields to clear the stones, to keep their land in good heart. Fields have to be won and, once won, maintained. It has been so for generations.

There's a hint of wealth in this impressive sea of hard hats at Storrs Hall, Windermere, seen during a cattle sale. In the crowd, just an occasional woman, perhaps only one, for in the main it is a male preserve. 'For Gentlemen Farmers', as posters of the time were fond of saying. One well-known Lakeland face is caught on the left-hand side of the ring, in top hat, cravat and holding a sale list — Thomas Longmire in old age, the renowned Cumberland and Westmorland wrestler. Cattle and sheep sales were and are a way of life in the Lake counties, though not all were so grand as this. Farm sales, too, could draw big crowds and often meant that the seller provided generous quantities of food for prospective buyers, as well as for the cannier elements who turned up just for eats. It certainly used to happen.

Opposite:
It's milking time, and farmer Wilson Martin of Mosedale House near Mungrisdale gives the cat a drop of milk. Here she sits, open mouthed, as he squirts in a fresh, warm drink straight from source. Hard to see but definitely there, Wilson's daughter is said to have taught the cat this one.

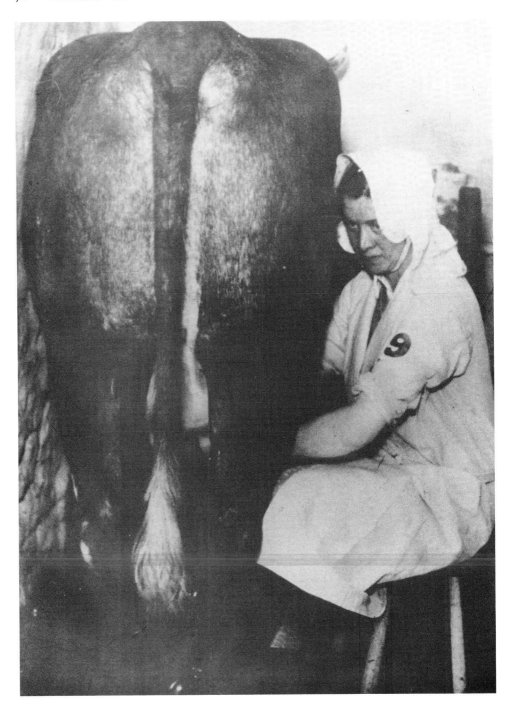

Milking time again. A woman student in overall and hood learns how to milk a cow by hand. Modern milking machines were probably mostly a dream when this picture was taken at Newton Rigg Farm School, near Penrith.

The school started in the 1890s — a second farming college, Aspatria Agricultural College, was also functioning, but of the two establishments only Newton Rigg was to survive. It came into existence following the passing of the 1889 Technical Instruction Act with the start of systematic farm education in Britain.

At Aspatria the success of the Travelling Dairy School had caught the imagination of many, and the idea grew that a fixed dairy school and experimental farm were definitely needed. Soon a strong lobby developed to set up a joint Westmorland, Cumberland and Northumberland farm school, though Northumberland dropped out.

Elsewhere, a host of people were in the struggle to create Newton Rigg, including technical lecturers, county councillors and even the famous champion of Cumbrian causes, Canon Hardwicke Rawnsley. Eventually they were successful and, when set up, it cost £7,000 and included a farm of 116 acres (52ha), a house, outbuilding and two cottages.

The first two women students began in September 1896. Two months later, eight men started. The plan was to teach systematic dairy work to women in the summer, and in the winter general farming to young men who already worked on farms. When the first nervous groups of farmers' sons came straight off the land, an equally watchful staff was quickly relieved to find that the lads were 'quite the right sort'. Students' lessons ranged from farming science in the mornings, to butter making in the afternoons. Then they were loaded up with homework. A regular grumble was that it was easier work back at home on the farm than it was at the school.

All is spick and span in the butter dairy at Newton Rigg Farm School. Pupils and teacher stand amid an array of butter churns. If the pupils hadn't strong arms at this stage, they would have before long.

A Cumberland pig is held fast by a cord at a West Cumbrian farm while the man with the poleaxe stands ready to strike the death blow. The young gilt had probably already had a litter before this fateful day. Many cottagers fattened a pig as a necessary means of keeping everyone fed, though less-well-off families might resort to a goose or hens. At the appropriate times, butchers went round the farms and cottages. One accurate swing to the head with the poleaxe would bring the pig crashing.

In the stony heart of the mountains, dalesman farmer John Richardson pauses at Stockley Bridge above Seathwaite in Borrowdale, a Herdwick hogg across the back of his pony. Mr Richardson farmed Seathwaite Farm and, like Ned Nelson of Gatesgarth, was renowned for the high quality of his Herdwick flocks. Shepherding on ponies was not uncommon and made for an easier lift back if a sheep were in need of urgent attention down at the farm.

Thomas Bewley, shepherd, on Dunmail Raise. He lived at Raise Cottage and this picture, which was used in the original *Lakeland Pedlar* of 1974, is here now because many people have written to say it was always their favourite. One family from Marton, near Ulverston, recognised Thomas as a relation, and sure enough this picture was hanging on a wall in their farm.

The lamb he is holding is a Herdwick, a native of the Cumbrian fells. Remarkably, these and other mountain sheep as a rule stay on their own pastures, or native *heafs,* needing no walls or fences to keep them to their traditional grazing ground. At times, perhaps in severe weather, or if scared by stray dogs, a ewe will find itself on a strange heaf, where sooner or later a shepherd will know it by its ear or *smit* marks as another man's property. Each year at shepherds' meets, a sorting out of strays ensues. Long ago the meet was used to define boundaries, settle fell rights of pasturage, and any disputes about such rights. So strong is the heafing instinct, among Herdwicks for example, that sheep sold from one farm to another have maddeningly been known to walk all the way back to their original owner, sometimes taking weeks to do so. A well-known story of a Herdwick ewe Back o' Skiddaw tells that it walked home three times before the exasperated new owner admitted defeat and sold it back into its original farm. Even lambs quickly pick up attachment to their own heaf. 'Where the lamb sucks, there it will be', is the saying.

Stock, Crop, &c., for Sale.

To be Sold

By Public Auction, under a Bill of Sale,

On Friday, the 26th of December, 1856,

AT

HEWER-HILL

In the Parish of Castle Sowerby, Cumberland,

THE FOLLOWING

STOCK, CROP

&c.,

Consisting of 1 Spring Calving Cow, 1 Bullock, rising 2 years old; 1 useful work Mare; 1 Spring Feeding Shot; 2 Brood Geese and 1 Gander.

CROP.—3 Stacks of Wheat, 3 do. of Oats, 1 do. of Lea Hay, 500 stones of Lea Hay, by stone, 1200 stones of Meadow Hay, and a quantity of Wheat and Barley Straw, by the score, a quantity of Potatoes, by stone.

HUSBANDRY & DAIRY UTENSILS, &c.—2 Carts and Cart gear, 1 Iron Plough and Ploughing gear, 1 Pair of Harrows, 1 Cheese Press, 1 Curd Mill and all the rest of the Husbandry and Dairy Utensils.

ALSO, ALL THE

HOUSEHOLD FURNITURE

Consisting of Beds, Bedsteads and Bedding, Clock, Chest of Drawers, Corner Cupboards, long Settles, Chairs, Pots, Pans, Crockery Ware, and various other Articles.

Conditions will be made known at the time of Sale, which will commence at 1 o'Clock precisely.

J. Armstrong, Auctioneer.

JAMES FOSTER, PRINTER, CARLISLE.

Women in elegant clothes pause to watch farmer Robert Jackson and his son Thomas clipping sheep at Syke Farm, Buttermere. The women were all members of Harrington Wesleyan Church and were on an outing into rural Cumberland with the intention of seeing wool at its source, the subject of a sermon given earlier in the year.

…atɪoɪi
Killarney.

BERRIER

Mr. Stephenson's annual clipping at Berrier was attended by 33 experienced clippers, along with catchers, markers and fleecers, so that an immense number of sheep were deprived of their fleeces. A party of 70 sat down to supper in Mr. Stephenson's spacious kitchen, where toasts included the "Host and hostess" and "The oldest clipper". The proceedings were interspersed by songs, delivered in excellent style by the best local talent. The gathering broke up about 2 o'clock with *Auld Lang Syne*.

GARRIGILL

The half-yearly meeting ⸗ he managers of Ga⸗

Berrier 100 years ago, from the *Cumberland and Westmorland Herald*.

Man with a scythe, man with a rake, man with the mower. A haytiming team at Godmans Hall Farm, Burneside, Kendal.

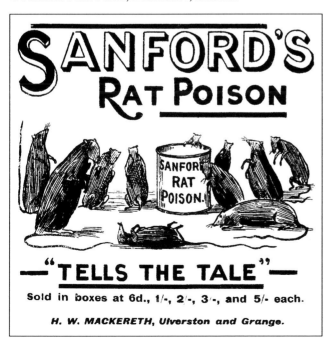

From the *Furness Year Books*, printed in Ulverston. These annual publications were read as much for their mix of advertisements as for their calendar of events, *Annals of Our Time.* The adverts ranged from tic pills to foot rot treament, from gout and rheumatic cures to lung tonic, from worm balls to boxes of rat poison.

The hired woman has brought the men and the lads their drinks out to the fields at Brigsteer for the 'ten o'clocks', and so for a few minutes the harrowing and the rolling stop for the morning break. A tin bottle or can of tea and a slice and a half of bread were customary.

Sometimes during the day, unofficial stops for a cigarette might occur. 'Nay, what if the master comes?' the youngest lad would wail. 'Never fear, we'll know', was the answer. And sure enough when the master appeared the cigarette had disappeared, work was under way and the lad was mystified. 'Next time, watch the horse's head', the lad was advised. Little flicks sharper than the ears of a horse.

Opposite:
Six skilfully thatched corn stacks near the Abbey Hotel, Barrow-in-Furness. It is February, and the trees are bare and a load of turnips is ready for feeding to the stock.

A good man might take three days to produce one of these beautifully finished stacks. Twisted straw ropes bind the tops and the sides have been trimmed. The corn, probably oats, has still to be thrashed, whenever the feed is needed.

Great pride was taken in stack building. In the evenings, at the local pub or in the reading room, they would be the subject of critical discussion among other farm-workers. Sundays would see men take time to walk round and eye up the finished work, appreciating the straightness of the lines and the care shown in the waterproof tops. This pride extended to other aspects of farming. A well-laid hedge, a well-hung gate, a field well ploughed. A man with his horse team who could produce straight furrows was reckoned to know his job — a true craftsman.

Come harvest time, just about everybody lent a hand. Back in 1909 when the oats were being cut at Cowran Farm, Pennington, Ulverston, all the Bell family turned out to help father and the hired hands, from grandmother down to the youngest able child. Nothing was wasted, and at such times the children were set to gather in every scattered scrap.

Threshing day at Speelbank Farm, Cartmel. The womenfolk have brought refreshments for the threshers. The noisy steam machines seemed to be the peak of modernity — it is after all 1913 — yet even these would one day be consigned to the museums.

Some Criminal Goings On

I T'S THE *Police Gazette* from years ago and was found in Ulverston when a police station was sold. Leading the page with 'Wanted for Murder — ~£50 reward' is one William Ward, slightly bald on the top of his head, very quarrelsome when in drink, drooping shoulders, walks badly. 'Now thought to be visiting Race Meetings in the Provinces.' Not Carlisle or Cartmel, we trust.

At Barrow-in-Furness, Arthur M, age thirty-one, is wanted for burglary; at Cockermouth, Matthew S, age twenty-seven, stole two bottles of spirits; and at Penrith, William J, age thirty two is reported to have vanished, along with a ton of coal. Police descriptions are terse, often graphic:

For carnally knowing a girl under sixteen years of age, Andrew T, laundry collector. A rather large forehead, sallow, thinning brown hair, drooping moustache, dark sympathetic eyes, scar on top of head, an inveterate cigarette smoker.

For obtaining a baby's nightgown, Mary or May W, domestic servant. Pinched face, eyes dark, bad teeth, pointed chin, thin body, addicted to drink.

THE POLICE GAZETTE
PUBLISHED BY AUTHORITY.

WANTED FOR MURDER.
£50 REWARD.
METROPOLITAN POLICE DISTRICT.

1.—T Division.—Portrait and description of WILLIAM WARD, wanted for wilful murder at Chiswick, 28th October, 1908, age 30, (looks older), height 5 ft. 7 or 8 ins., complexion fresh, eyes grey, hair dark brown (grey at sides, slightly bald on top of head), thin face, high cheek bones, aquiline or Roman nose, drooping moustache ginger, may now be clean shaved or growing a beard, slight build, drooping shoulders, splay footed, walks badly. This man is still at large and believed to be in this country, may now be found visiting Race Meetings in the Provinces, or travelling the country with a horse and cart, as a dealer in old rubber, &c., is very quarrelsome when in drink, and may at any time be charged with drunkenness or fighting. See Special Notice "Police Gazette," 5th March, 1909, Case No. 2, 13th, and No. 5, 20th November, 1908.

The above reward will be paid by Mr. H. W. Hardy, 279, High! Road, Chiswick, London, W., to any person giving such information as will lead to the apprehension and conviction of the above.

Information to be forwarded to the Metropolitan Police Office, New Scotland Yard, London, S.W.

For obtaining food (pies) by false pretences, Arthur B, showman's labourer. Eyes blue, two grey patches on top of head, check jacket splashed with lime wash, blue trousers, brown lace boots, patched on soles with leather belting.

For obtaining a pair of boots by false pretences, Charles R, dust carter, age forty to forty-five, eyes brown, hook nose, one left upper tooth missing, stoops slightly, grey trousers (very tight fitting, and split at back), lace boots (size eight, new, slightly nailed).

A tough lot, indeed. Convictions varied from two months in jail for shop breaking at Whitehaven, to six weeks for stealing a shirt in Kendal.

Charles H------: factory operative. Aged sixteen. Marks: two blue dots on right arm, one on left arm; and one between forefinger and thumb on both hands. Convictions: 31st October 1884, Kendal borough: stealing 3s 6d from a shop — ten days' gaol. Offences elsewhere: for stealing 3s from a shop — discharged, prosecutor declined to prosecute. Sedbergh: stealing 4lb of tobacco. Discharged.

John C-----: horse dealer. Aged fifty. Eyes grey, large nose, hair dark brown. Marks: scar right side of forehead and bridge of nose. Red bloated face. Ears sticking out. Convictions: at Kendal, for obtaining money by false pretence, five years' penal servitude, five years' police supervision. Offences else- where include: stealing brush, seven days' hard labour; embezzlement, two months' HL; obtaining money by false pretence, six months HL; larceny, seven years' penal servitude, seven years' supervision; stealing a horse, twelve months' HL.

George M-------: Barber. Aged sixty-two. Eyes hazel, hair brown, turning grey. Marks: bracelet tattooed left wrist. Ring tattooed second and third fingers of left hand. Large scar front of ear, back of head and back of neck. Nose flat; has been broken. Convictions: at Kendal, drunkenness, fined 3s; assault, twenty-one days.

George G----: Labourer, Aged thirty-six. Eyes grey, hair light brown. Marks: large toe joint right foot. Convictions: found on enclosed premises with intent to commit felony, Kendal, twenty-one days. Other offences include begging and obscene language, seven and fourteen days HL; drunk and disorderly, one month HL; destroying his clothes in the Union, fourteen days; stealing vest and braces, one month.

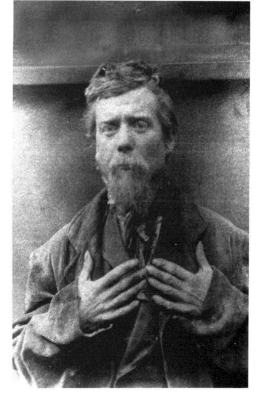

He was once the most hunted person in Britain. For three months the search for Percy Francis Toplis made the headlines in the nation's newspapers. The former First World War soldier was wanted on one charge of murder, and on two charges of alleged murder. For long enough it seemed that he would never be caught. But in June 1920, the police set up an ambush near Penrith knowing that the hunted man was walking towards them. Both the police and the runaway were armed.

Toplis was alleged to have shot dead a Salisbury taxi driver in a field near Andover, Hampshire. The inquest verdict was that the driver was killed by an ex-soldier — named Toplis. The search began, with intensive manhunts in places that Toplis had never even visited so that gradually other murders were attributed to him, including that of a nurse on a train to the south coast, as well as killings in a Cornish town.

Toplis fled into Scotland, where he hid in a deserted hunting lodge. When challenged, he shot and wounded a policeman and a gamekeeper before heading south, eventually reaching Cumberland. Daringly he spent a night as a casual guest in the Border Regiment depot at Carlisle Castle, then he set out on the 6th June 1920 for Penrith on his last walk. He trekked for miles down the A6 before he attracted the attention of PC Isaac Fulton of Low Hesket. The constable, while suspicious, was unsure about the stranger's identity and let him go, but once home he checked the wanted list and guessed that it was the hunted man. He set off on his bike in pursuit.

As he caught up with Toplis, the runaway drew a revolver and said: 'It's me you are looking for? If you are, I am the man; I'm Toplis.' And later he said: 'It was me who shot the policeman and the keeper — and if you act the same, you go too.' He ordered the unarmed constable to throw down his handcuffs and truncheon, then enigmatically he let Fulton go, vowing: 'I'll kill, or be killed.' Then he ran off across the fields.

An urgent phone call from Fulton to the chief constable resulted in an armed police ambush being set up further

Percy Toplis — ambushed and shot dead. A Sam Brown outfit, but was he really a commissioned officer?

down his apparent route. As Toplis headed towards Penrith, the police confronted him at Romanway, near Plumpton, and he turned and ran, firing twice. He was still running when the police fired and he fell dead, shot through the heart.

There is a great deal more than this to the story of Toplis, including his part in the British Army rebellion at Étaples, south of Boulogne, in the mutiny of 1917 during which British troops sought better conditions.

The runaway was given a pauper's funeral at Penrith. Hordes of journalists and photographers arrived to record the burial, but the police outwitted them, announcing a different burial time from the real one, and the ceremony took place in secret. A lorry, which normally carried mineral water, was used discreetly as the Toplis hearse; and his coffin was plain deal. The grave was unmarked, though down the years, just occasionally, a few flowers used to appear there.

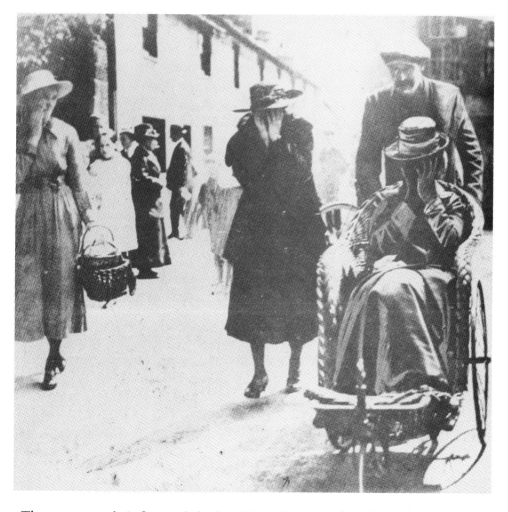

Three women, their fingers skeletal and haunting, seen after the inquest in Penrith of Percy Toplis. The woman in the wheelchair is Toplis's mother, heartbroken. The others appear to be a companion and a passer-by caught up in the tragedy of the moment.

A Few of the Natives

SOMETIMES YOU WILL hear people say that there are no characters around in Lakeland anymore, not when compared with the old days. Whether that is true or not, there are certainly a few of the natives who come close to qualifying.

From long ago first ... there's a delightful remarkable gingerbread maker included here, and a man, who was once well known in Cumberland at least (and, in his day, even by Selfridges in London) whose fame rested partly on the shirts he sold, as well as on his ability to advertise intelligently.

Another person still mentioned is Ruddy Mary. Year in year out she walked the Cumbrian roads pushing a pram loaded with rudd stone to sell to farms and cottages. Mary is believed to be the woman sitting at the foot of the market cross in the Carlisle picture, included a little further on, so perhaps she does appear.

Here too are more pictures of Beatrix Potter which have come to light. She did not start out as a Cumbrian native but she certainly became one and was well liked by the farming community especially.

And what of today? Tales are told of a former Lakeland landlord who was stabbed in the arm by his enraged girlfriend, and who calmly responded to her waving knife by pouring a pint of beer over her head, followed by a second pint, grabbed off the bar.

Elsewhere, in a small hilltop village, an enraged farmer chased his wife down the road brandishing an axe (which luckily never reached her). He ended by falling into a midden where she sat on him and where eventually both ended up drinking a bottle of whisky (some versions say gin). Is it true? Well, it's a good story.

Less dramatic, though engaging, was an enterprising teenager. Each dustbin day, before the dustmen arrived, he woke early, toured the neighbourhood and raided his neighbours' bin bags and throw-outs for any treasures. He was not identified for long enough, though his home apparently featured a rare range of belongings, including a giant set of antlers over the kitchen stove which by chance their former owner recognised.

My own favourite is that of the mysterious person who occasionally marches down the main street of a lakeside town in the middle of the night playing *Amazing Grace* on bagpipes. He or she has never been captured by the local constabulary, though at the last report they were still hopeful.

Probably in years to come people will still be saying, just as you hear sometimes now, that there are no characters any more, just ordinary Cumbrians.

Millican Dalton was called the Professor of Adventure, and if only half the tales about this delightful and eccentric man are true, then he deserves the title. He was a man who achieved his simplest and his greatest wish, a life out of doors.

He lived during the summers in his cave at the heart of Lakeland, at Castle Crag in Borrowdale, where visitors were entertained with lively, lucid conversations; or joined him on rock-climbing expeditions; or were whisked away on sudden treks to explore the high fells.

Millican was born in 1867 at Nenthead beyond Alston and he was educated at the Friends' School in Wigton. As a young man he was an insurance clerk in a London office, but the world of commerce was not for him and when thirty or so years old he left it all behind in a momentous decision, turning to a life as a professional mountain guide and camper. At first, in 1905, he led organised tours in Scotland, the Lake District and Switzerland, managing to live on a tiny income. He climbed the Matterhorn and created something of a sensation by starting mixed tours for campers. For a while, too, he was a guide for the Holiday Fellowship in Borrowdale.

He camped a great deal in the valley he had chosen to make his home, and settled for the cave in the picture overleaf, at House Quarry. The Lake District surely never had a more colourful mountain guide. In Tyrolean hat and blue wool round his ankles, he pushed a bicycle with a blue frame along Borrowdale's narrow roads, a kind of Robinson Crusoe figure, all manner of goods hanging from his machine, which he frequently used more as a wheelbarrow. He did not wear socks, it is said, but only the tops. And if his jacket was ragged at the edges, he was himself always tidy and clean. He enjoyed being called 'Professor of Adventure', and it was also true that he was a 'Gentleman of the Hills'. Kindly, modest, courteous, intelligent he was all of these, and was regarded by many with considerable affection.

Millican was a good climber and a safe leader on rock climbs, as many novices testified. He never took undue risks, climbing well within his limits. On the heights, he most enjoyed Great Gable's western side, the Needle, which he scaled many times, and Slingsby's chimney on Scafell.

After a long day on the fells, he loved to return to his cave which was a haven of comfort. He did not believe in roughing it. He walled in one part as living quarters. In one corner was his bracken bed, often changed, and a plaid blanket which he enjoyed wearing out of doors as

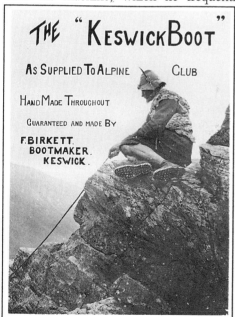

THE "KESWICK BOOT"

AS SUPPLIED TO ALPINE   CLUB

HAND MADE THROUGHOUT

GUARANTEED AND MADE BY

F. BIRKETT.
BOOTMAKER.
KESWICK.

Millican Dalton, as many people first saw him. His photograph in this Keswick Boot advertisement was a permanent part of the scene in that town before the First World War, advertising Birkett's boots, which he himself wore.

Millican smokes contentedly by his fire while a visitor reads him the latest news. He smoked his cigarettes down to the last gasp, spiking each stub on a pin so that nothing was wasted.

well as in. And he used an eiderdown, his comfort and joy. He had his own seat, built beside the fire, fresh water in a pool and all manner of hanging gadgets for keeping his belongings tidy. He was a vegetarian with a passion for coffee, and he smoked heavily. It was a great sight to see Millican, blue eyed and tanned, sitting contentedly by his camp fire, the flames dancing on the rock walls, a cigarette lodged between his big toe of his right foot, while he sewed at a tent flap, or mused as he puffed away at a cigarette which he smoked down to the end, using a pin. His motto faced you as you stepped into his cave, cut into the rock:'Don't! Waste Words, Jump to Conclusions!'

Millican was one of the pioneers of the lightweight approach to life outdoors: he kept everything to the minimum. He made and sold tents, rucksacks and camping gear of his own design.

One of his pleasures was raft building. They were usually odd structures and some of them not oversafe — he was plunged into Derwentwater on one memorable occasion at least. He fitted them with small sails and journeyed out into the wide waters of the lake, often watched by amused and admiring sightseers.

As time passed, he spent his winters in the milder south of England, at Epping Forest, still camping, still the outdoor man. He died when he was eighty years old. Fire destroyed his forest dwelling and he took a chill in a temporary tent; and it turned to pneumonia.

To all the stories I can add one more, from 1974, when one of his nephews, Robert Dalton, who was seventy-two, wrote from Woodford Wells in Essex:

'He was my father's youngest brother, and a great favourite with us children in the period pre-1914. He came to stay with us, mainly in the winters and I can still recall the distinctive camp-fire smell of Uncle Millican's den up in the attic, to which he encouraged us boys to follow his example by ascending the three floors on the outside of the building by rope ladder …'

Above all else, Millican Dalton had style.

Millican catches up with the news outside a Keswick shop. The Second World War was
on and walking sticks now cost 1s 3d (6½p) each; Hitler is news, and *The Times* newsboard
advises on growing food in wartime. Millican seems more interested in the local
Lake District Herald.

Time for a gossip at Carlisle Cross. It's market day and the two ragged women are selling *rudd stone*, popular with many housewives who used it to give their doorsteps and window surrounds a coating of red. The woman with rolled sleeves is believed to be Ruddy Mary. Many people knew her in Cumberland. She dug up the stone from riverbeds, and for years, accompanied by her husband or her son, she would load up an old pram with the stone and set off to push it for miles along country lanes to farms and cottages, selling the rudd for a few pence as she went. Sometimes she took her dog with her. Mary would lead the way with the pram, the dog sitting on top of the heap, and her son followed behind in his long trailing coat. She walked the rural roads for years, and even today many can still tell stories of Ruddy Mary.

Mrs Heelis, better known as the children's author Beatrix Potter, is interviewed for a BBC programme at the 1933 Woolpack Show, Eskdale. The author lived at Hill Top, Near Sawrey, Hawkshead, and here the interviewer is Harry Lamb, of Caldbeck, a writer, broadcaster and farmer.

William Heelis, country solicitor, at Near Sawrey, Hawkshead. He and Beatrix were married in October, 1913, at St Mary Abbot's Parish Church, Kensington, London.

Beatrix Potter took many photographs, and among them is the one shown here. The boy, Albert Richard Bunting, of Far Sawrey, remembered that he was eight when he was snapped. Albert recalled that the photo was used as the model for one of the author's drawings in *The Tale of Pigling Bland* …

Aye, this was taken by Beatrix Potter and it's with our local grocer, Mr Fleming, of Sawrey, and I'm handing Mr Fleming … noo, I believe Mr Fleming's handing me a bottle of medicine, to take to Beatrix Potter's. It was taken 1912. And I'm the pig in Pigling Bland, *apparently.*

It's taken in the farmyard at Beatrix Potter's land. The horse was called Joey. Mr Fleming's first name was William, a grocers and provision merchants in those days. This photo she used to get the drawing off in the book. I was eight years old when the picture was taken. I can't remember her taking this picture, but she often took photos. She was not very fond of children. No, she wasn't.

[Mr Bunting's wife, Anne, remembered the photograph]

We had it given when Flemings were clearing out the house. They were going to burn it. One of the daughters gave it when turning the drawers out. Said 'Here you are, Anne, it's got Albert on it.'

Mrs Mary Agnes Rogerson, left, housekeeper and cook to Beatrix Potter, and Mrs Sarah Benson, the daily help, with the author's dogs outside Castle Cottage, Sawrey. Mrs Rogerson remembered working for Beatrix Potter ...

The old woman, Mrs Heelis ... I was with her for thirty-six years and I'll say this right off, she was all right to work for; she never bothered you. Sometimes I hardly ever saw her. As long as my work was done, and the meals was there for her, that's all she cared about. She was very easy with her food.

She was very quaint. At first I could make nothing of her hardly. I got the job with her through my mother-in-law. She was a great friend of hers.

With children — well, she didn't care all that much about children. It's funny, you know, when she could write those books. And I've seen her when she'd have nothing to do with children. She took a lot of photographs. But they've got squandered.

Well she used to work with a candle. Aye, it's a wonder she never set herself afire many a time. She would be working having a candle burning and it would get on to her forehead and it would get singed a few times. She wouldn't have electricity. As soon as she died Mr Heelis put electricity in. She didn't like the wireless. She didn't like modern things whatever. She used to say wireless and electricity, it was the work of the devil. No television. But she'd go and watch it at other people's houses if there was anything she wanted to see special. But she wouldn't have it in her own house whatever. She'd often say to me, she says: 'Come on, Mrs Rogerson', she says, 'we'll go and watch something special next door'.

Her clothes ... well, they're rather funny to explain. Tweed. A coarse apron made out of her own sheep's' wool. She was proud to use her own sheep, especially Herdwick. Oh she loved the sheep, and sheep dogs and all that sort of thing, but sheep was her speciality. She didn't make her own clothes herself. My sister-in-law used to make a lot for her, Mrs Jessie Brockbank, lived next door to me in Sawrey.

She paid sixpence [2½p] a day. Yes, it's true, that was when I started.

I started as a daily help. She had another housekeeper at first. But eventually I became the housekeeper. I started in 1914, something like that, pay sixpence a day. It wasn't much. It didn't take much spending I tell you in them days. She never asked me to do anything, she just let me have my own way. I never had a row with her.

But Tommy Christopherson, he used to drive a lorry for her. Well he was one for telling her off. Tommy wasn't particular what he said to her. Tommy was always saying: 'Give us me cards, give us me cards.' That was what he was saying. And she'd say: 'If I do, you'll only lose them.' They were comical at times.

Tom Nanson of Bowscales, Mungrisdale, is not of the 1900 period, he's more modern than that, but the stories about him capture the old way of Lakeland as much as anything does.

'Can you tell us the way to Berrier?' he was asked. The hamlet lay a couple of miles away. 'Aye', he advised, 'with a spee-add.'

He was as droll as folk come. One thing, he did not enjoy people trying it on with money.

'Nay, you owe us a half crown', Tom told an employer.

'Aye?' The man's face screwed up a bit. 'Well here's a penny for thee — same size, same shape but a different colour.'

'Is that right?' said Tom. 'Then here's a black eye for nowt.'

Road gang foremen seemed to see Tom as a natural target.

'And just which way do you reckon these cockeyed pipes of yours will start to flow?' said one, scowling into a trench of Tom's drainage efforts.

'Downhill, you silly ******', said Tom.

Arms folded and the centrepiece of one of his own once-famous advertisements is the Sark MP, Sir William Moffitt. *Sark* is Cumbrian for shirt, and if one man knew how to sell them then it was William.

He was one of Carlisle's best known businessmen, who founded a thriving shirt sales and outfitting enterprise with three shops in the city. His advertisements were considered to be years ahead of their time, and often were so novel that even Selfridges of London offered him a job as publicity agent, a post he politely declined. Of course William Moffitt was neither MP nor Sir, they were tags partly self-generated, though also generously accorded by many of his customers who enjoyed the joke.

Besides selling his famous sarks, William was an energetic supporter of good causes, and especially the old Hethersgill Methodist Chapel for which he raised much of the building money. He did so by persuading farmers to donate sheep which he sold at auction in Carlisle.

He died in 1923 and it is said that he was buried in unconsecrated ground outside the Hethersgill chapel's front door, for that is where his family thought he would be happiest. However, he did not stay there. The premises were turned into an arts centre. On a moonlit night, the body of the Sark MP was lifted in his coffin and he was reinterred in consecrated ground.

He may not seem other than an ordinary Cumbrian, but Old Will Ritson of Wasdale Head gained the reputation of being the greatest storyteller and the sharpest wit in all Lakeland. For many years the Wastwater Hotel became a haven for the climbing world, and it was Will who helped to bring that about.

He was born in 1808 at Row Foot, Wasdale Head, when it was a small farmstead. He was passionate about hunting and his resulting deep knowledge of the fells turned him to hiring himself out as a mountain guide, and to cater for the mountain men. To this end he extended his farmhouse, obtained a drinks licence and named it the Huntsman Inn, later to become the Wastwater Hotel. Into Will's flagged kitchen with its rough benches came the shepherds, the farmers, the guides and especially the daring young men, the new enthusiastic breed of rock climbers, often attracted by Will's reputation as a mountain man.

Will's other reputation was as the world's biggest liar, a title he enjoyed, and to that end he delivered his tall stories with the utmost gravity.

'Canst see that flea on t'mountain, Will?'

'Aye', said Will. 'It just winked.'

'And who', said a judge at a lying competition, 'can tell the biggest lie?'

'I've never told a lie yet', said Will, who won.

To this day the saying is that Wasdale had the deepest lake, the highest mountain, the smallest church and the biggest liar.

In his youth Will was a powerful wrestler and once had a tremendous encounter with the redoubtable Christopher North, himself a skilled combatant. Will, tall, active and athletic, threw North twice out of three rounds, something that delighted North who was never one to begrudge a fair defeat.

As to Will, when it came to being Cumbrian he got a good start from his father Old John Ritson, as on the day they dropped in at the Kirk Stile Inn at Loweswater. Will charged his father's glass, saying (though in dialect) 'You must say when, father'.

He poured away but the old man never said, and Will poured some more and still he never said, and Will stopped only when the glass overflowed.

'You never said when', he remonstrated.

'Nay, that's right', said Old John. 'A lucky man may make his fortune by holding his tongue.'

If Sarah Nelson locks a pretty severe woman it is understandable enough, because she certainly had a hard life. She was born as Sarah Kemp in Bowness-on-Windermere in 1815 and as a child, with her widowed mother, knew the meaning of poverty. She worked in service and learned to be a cook, and in 1844 married Wilfred Nelson, a labourer and part-time gravedigger of Morland, near Penrith. They had little money, and with two daughters to support, they struggled to survive. Sarah took in washing, and started to make cakes and pastries for Lady Farquhar, at Dale Lodge, Grasmere.

When the village's former school, Gate Cottage, became rentable, they moved in, at the corner of the churchyard of St Oswald's, and it was there that Sarah was encouraged by Lady Farquhar's French chef to try her hand at baking gingerbread. It was a lucky idea. Sarah sat out in the cobbled yard and sold the gingerbread to passing Victorian tourists, and from this modest beginning her Grasmere gingerbread became renowned. Her recipe became a closely guarded secret and was kept in the vault of a local bank.

Tragedy came later when the Nelsons' daughters died of tuberculosis in 1869-70, and a few years later Wilfred also died. Sarah, in her own way a tough lady, lived until 1904, when she was eighty-eight. The little gingerbread shop is still going strong.

Poor old Freddie Cairns — he married a tartar. Even the magistrates thought so. If he looks a bit downcast, it must be because he was fond of rummaging in dustbins, or perhaps it is just the photograph because kindly Freddie, it was said, never harmed a soul. His main stamping grounds were Cockermouth and Workington, where he roamed the streets selling paper windmills to children.

But the day came when Freddie did the unexpected and got married. His bride, a buxom lass called Mary Moore, already the mother of two, tipped his life upside-down. For a start, she let the penniless Freddie walk home to Workington from the register office in Cockermouth while she went off by train for tea with a friend. And within a couple of months she was jailed at Carlisle for letting one of her children beg in the streets.

'You had nearly better put a rope round your neck, Freddie', the magistrates' chairman told him, 'than to have wed.'

And poor Freddie could only agree that he had made a bad match. Despite the drastic change in his life, he remained a favourite in Workington, loved at least by the children.

A royal handshake. Bob Hanvey of Aspatria, grand old man of Cumbrian rugby union, is introduced to King George V at Twickenham in 1926. Bob had made the England trials in 1921 and again in 1924, and then in 1926 he received his velvet cap. In that last year he played in all four of the international games, against France, Scotland, Wales, and Ireland. Two games were won, two lost. Bob, first as a player, then as a referee and finally as an official, achieved a remarkable active involvement with rugby union which lasted for seventy years.

Men and women in black. Well wrapped, and all wearing headgear, a solemn line-up of the natives at Braithwaite, near Keswick.

Annie Nelson of Gatesgarth, Buttermere, nurses a young fox. The fox had been saved by Annie from a hunt, and it slept with her dog in a shed and she cared for it for eighteen years. Annie was renowned for providing farmhouse teas, a practice appreciated down the years by many thousands of fellwalkers. Writers, artists and poets made a point of visiting Annie. Beatrix Potter looked in and sat by the glowing iron range and had tea. Queen Wilhelmina of the Netherlands called when on a sketching visit. In her own way, Annie was famous. The Nelson family was well known in other ways, too. Her grandfather, Old Ned Nelson and her father, Young Ned, were renowned for their prize-winning Herdwick sheep.

Sometimes a picture turns up and no one knows a thing about it. And sometimes there are people who definitely know all about it, though the stories differ. This is the picture of a midwife who worked in and around Windermere. No one could tell of her name for sure, but a copy of the same picture turned up in Carlisle, and no one there could exactly tell her name, though she was said to be an old farmer's wife and not a midwife, and the only children in her life had been six of her own. And then another real explanation came to light, that her name was Margaret Longmire of Troutbeck, and that a similar picture to this was taken in 1864 to celebrate her hundredth birthday and the *Westmorland Gazette* reported at the time that she was still in good health. So that must surely be right? Whichever is correct, she stares at us out of the past with an expression too powerful to ignore.

The cultured man who turned wild. Lakeland has probably never seen a more unusual fellow than the Skiddaw Hermit. He was a Scotsman called George Smith, and he lived in a strange wickerwork den on Skiddaw Dodd during the 1860s.

In Keswick he was known as the Dodd Man. Children sometimes mocked him as he tramped past, staff in hand. And parents soon learned to threaten their offspring with: 'Behave, or I'll get the Skiddaw Hermit to you!'

George was born in Banffshire in 1825, moving to the Lake District when almost forty. He was tall, had black hair, and went hatless and barefooted in tattered clothes, a cultured man gone wild. It was said he had retreated to the Lakes because of a soured love affair and was determined to hide and heal his wound. Another account attributed his sudden nomadic life to the death of his parents.

At first he lodged in Keswick, frequently returning in mudstained clothes from long tramps, during which he slept rough in shepherd's huts. Then he built his strange den. It stood on a ledge in Scalebeck Gill up on the Dodd, a large basket-shaped structure of branches interlaced with bracken, and weatherproofed with grass and moss. There was a hole near the top for a doorway and inside was a bed of leaves, two boulders, one of which George used as a table, and a fire for cooking, though he cooked also on a tallow in a can. Wild though he was, he was said to be particular about keeping clean, washing his shirt in a beck and letting it dry on his back.

At intervals he descended into Keswick for food and drink, and apparently mainly the latter, for drink was said to be his curse. The hermit paid his way partly by painting watercolours and portraits in oils. He was an accomplished artist and good at a likeness. The two portraits shown below, of Hector and Harriet Bowe, who farmed at

Portraits of Hector and Harriet Bowe, of Mirkholme, Bassenthwaite,
attributed to the Skiddaw Hermit.

George Smith, the Skiddaw Hermit.

Mirkholm, Bassenthwaite, are attributed to George. Sometimes he moved from farm to farm or inn to inn painting portraits as he went, and often enough he was paid in food and drink. Other examples of his work are probably hanging in Lakeland farms and cottages today, their origins unrecognised, though one or two astute dealers are known to have done the rounds on the lookout.

Vandals out for a roister drove George from his Skiddaw den, causing him to move south to the Ambleside area where he slept out in a tent. His wild looks as much as anything got him into trouble with the police.

'Comical chase and capture of the Skiddaw Hermit.' Thus reported the *Carlisle Patriot* in March 1871. Poor George was described as being drunk and riotous in Ambleside. However, witnesses stated emphatically that he was not drunk, despite police and subsequent newspaper claims, and that the riot consisted of George shouting and waving his arms about, and getting excited when a crowd of children followed him around.

The actual chase came when friends coaxed him to court to answer the charges, but sight of waiting constables alarmed George and off he ran — in at the front door of the Troutbeck Bridge Inn and out at the back, down into the evergreens of a chapel, then away across a field with the constables hot in pursuit. He was caught in the end, of course, but with the majesty of the law thus gravely abused, George was sent to jail for seven days.

Yet the unexpected happened. At Bowness the hermit stopped to listen to a travelling preacher at the lakeside, and became a convert. The wild man who had lived in a wickerwork den, abstained from strong drink and bought a suit much like anyone else and, in the eyes of the locals, began to behave himself. In his own odd way he demonstrated his new outlook by cutting in half the front board of a Bible, and then did the same to the back. Shocked onlookers were reassured when he said that what had once been a closed work to him would now be an open book.

After memorable years in the Lake District, the hermit returned to Scotland, and later was admitted to an asylum and eventually hospital. George Smith, an unusual man who came in from the cold, lived until he was fifty.

Not quite the normal gateposts you would expect to find outside your home. These whale jawbones stood at Sunnyside, a house just over the railway bridge in West Silloth. Tradition has it that they are from a whale which was washed up near the town.

The photograph was taken in 1897. On the left is Mr Harry Barker who lived at Sunnyside and was the manager of *Maxwell's (later Fisons) Chemical Works*.

The boy, his son Arnold, became a bank clerk in Liverpool to which he travelled weekly by sea. Mr Barker was a talented amateur actor, and today his Silloth-born grandson, Tim Barker keeps the acting tradition going professionally, both on stage and in television.

Tommy Dobson, founder, huntsman and master of the Eskdale and Ennerdale Foxhounds, surveys the scene with William Porter, fourteen, who would follow in his steps.

Tommy is not the most famous huntsman — John Peel scores in that respect — yet his name seems to crop up whenever the Lakeland hunting fraternity meets for a good crack. Pictures of Tommy's genial face are always being found with Tommy following the hunt, nursing a fox cub or perhaps holding a tray laden with puppies.

A brisk, wiry little man, Tommy was from Staveley, Westmorland, and he set off to walk over the fells to Eskdale in western Lakeland, where he found work as a bobbin turner. His great delight was hunting and that was to prove popular with many of the farmers round him. Largely through Tommy's enthusiasm the Eskdale and Ennerdale Foxhounds was started, at a period when the founding of packs was almost exclusively the prerogative of wealthy individuals and landed proprietors. The bobbin-turner's resources were slender, but he managed to buy one or two hounds, and soon began to range the mountains round Eskdale after the foxes.

The farmers' interest grew, and little by little so did the pack, but it did so in the way Tommy wished, with no social elegance, or patronising subscribers, as he termed it. It was essentially a working hunt, intended for folk with strong legs and rough clothes. If the gentry wished to join in, he made them welcome, basing his respect on their hunting qualities.

The cost of keeping hounds proved to be a problem. A story was often told that in the early days he used to sacrifice his own breakfasts so that he could afford to buy food for his charges. In time, though, he gained more support from the farming community. He fed the hounds on oatmeal, and on sheep, cattle and horses that had died from natural causes. During the summers he boarded out the hounds among the farmers; and to encourage proper care, a prize was given at the annual Eskdale puppy show for the best boarded-out hound.

Tommy became master of the Eskdale and Ennerdale Foxhounds in 1857 and he followed the hunt for fifty-three years. To the dalesmen the hunt, as well as clearing the fells of foxes, became a kind of club, and farmers from miles around attended the hunt suppers, the main course of the evening being a steaming *tatie pot*.

In 1910, Tommy died in Little Lang- dale when the hunt was meeting there. He was eighty-three and had followed the pack until the end. His body was put in a coffin and loaded onto a horse- drawn trap. Accompanied by a cluster of mourners, the cortège set off in a slow trek for eight miles (13km) or so over the wilds of Wrynose and Hardknott passes to Eskdale (*see overleaf*). The journey took four hours, a string of people picking their way along the old stone road, umbrellas buffeted by wind and rain. At Eskdale a crowd of some 200 dalesmen met the cortège and a dark massed group carried the coffin at shoulder height to St Catherine's Church by the River Esk, where he was buried. Later a tombstone was put up carved with his likeness, along with the heads of a fox and a hound.

William Porter succeeded Tommy Dobson as master. For half a century Porter likewise hunted among the mountains, and he too died in harness, collapsing on Middle Fell, Wasdale, in 1952, and never regaining consciousness.

The master of Eskdale and Ennerdale Foxhounds, William Porter, with a lap full of fox cubs.

Tommy Dobson's funeral cart is lead round a hairpin bend on Hardknott Pass. A few wreaths deck the coffin, the showers have abated for now, and Eskdale lies below.

Tommy's coffin reaches Brook House Corner, Eskdale, and in its wake follows a mass of mourners.

The War to End all Wars

'HOME BY CHRISTMAS.' That was the hopeful cry of the men who went to war in 1914. Often it was cheerfully said. Many believed it. Few guessed at what lay ahead. At first, brave military music often accompanied the farewells. Parish magazines praised the young soldiers for their courageous attitude. The German emperor, Kaiser Wilhelm, was less impressed. He called Britain's first expeditionary force 'contemptible', a description which made the 'Old Contemptibles' inordinately proud.

Jingoism ruled. Field Marshal Kitchener's face appeared on 'Your Country Needs YOU' posters, famously pointing that accusing finger at everybody not in uniform. Everybody pleaded for everybody else to join up, including the earl of Lonsdale, though his poster 'Are you a Man or are you a Mouse?' did him no personal good.

Lakeland's Canon Rawnsley was among the many caught up in the excitement. In the early days of the war he used his considerable talent to some purpose. One of his fears was German infiltration into Britain. In a newspaper letter he claimed:

'There is a standing army of Germans in this country still, most of whom have been trained as soldiers, and many of whom have arms and ammunition in their lodgings.'

Scaring stuff. He warned about men with foreign accents, and whether it was the canon's warning alone, or that collectively of others, the Cumberland police swooped. The Germans were experts at coke-oven technology and most of the coke ovens in the Cumbrian iron smelting district still had German technicians to demonstrate how to work them. Arrests were made at Flimby and elsewhere. To the dismay of their Cumbrian wives and children, the husbands were sent to detention camps.

In fairness to the redoubtable canon, he was not alone in his fears. Much hysteria at the thought of spies was aroused in many parts of the country by numerous novels and plays. Then, as if a scene out of a film, a carload of suspicious foreigners appeared in Lakeland. Keswick police, bearing in mind the warning about accents, arrested them all. At once the town filled with rumours. German spies had been taken into custody. Townsfolk flocked to the police station to try to get a glimpse of the foreign agents. None was to be seen. The police were mortified to find they had arrested some touring Americans.

But spy fever grew. Reports came in to police stations that a plane had been heard, and later had been seen over the Lake District. Police and army units went on full alert. Armed search parties set out to hunt for intruders. Farmers and shepherds were warned to keep a sharp lookout, and to locate any oil and petrol stores. Soldiers of the 5th Battalion, the Border Regiment (TA), were mobilised at Cockermouth. Men of the Special Service Detachment set off on bikes into the fells to hunt for the spy plane. It was a serious business. All were armed with rifles loaded with ball cartridges. For a time Eskdale became the centre of attention. People there and at Wasdale said they had been hearing aeroplane noises at night. Accordingly, a newspaper correspondent wrote:

'There is reason to believe that a German aeroplane has been hiding for some days past in the fells around Eskdale ... visitors have seen it through the day resting on the fells.'

As rumours about the plane grew, reinforcements entered Lakeland from the Lancashire Fusiliers at Barrow-in-Furness, who mounted road blocks. Another armed force scoured the fells. More reports came of enemy planes flying at night. At Hesket Newmarket and Caldbeck a plane was reported to have been seen as well as heard. Boy Scout troops were stationed on mountain tops.

There was a final line of defence. At Workington, a Lieutenant Hicks was standing by with his Blériot aeroplane, apparently armed and ready. He had been engaged to give demonstration flights at Workington Sports, but he found himself 'mobilised'. A Cumbrian newspaper observed:

'We may all sleep soundly in our beds when Lieutenant Hicks is around to give us the benefit of his adequate protection'.

The lieutenant was never called upon to defend the local population. No German invaders were ever found. But the spy scare was real enough at the time.

And that might have seemed the last of the scares, though there were other developments. Daring bombardments took place by German U-boats on targets on the Cumbrian coast, and the war moved into the sky, itself, as Britain built a fleet of airships at Walney Island and elsewhere to hunt down the enemy.

SUBMARINES IN IRISH SEA.

THREE BRITISH MERCHANT SHIPS BLOWN UP BY THE GERMANS.

A start has now evidently been made by Admiral von Tirpitz with his policy of using the submarine against British merchant shipping.

On Saturday a German submarine, the U 21, appeared in the Irish Sea and sank three small merchantmen.

In each case the crew was given ten minutes to leave their ship, and after they had taken their boats, mines were placed on board and the vessel was blown up.

Mid-Cumberland and North Westmorland Herald

Rifles over shoulders, drummers leading the way, troops of the Lonsdale Battalion
attract a crowd of spectators during a recruiting march through High Street, Wigton.
It is still only 1915. By the end of the First World War in 1918, the town's death toll was
to amount to more than a hundred people.

August 1914, and the fate of these fine horses has been decided: they are about to be
loaded into the waiting train at Cark in Cartmel and taken to the war front in Europe.
They had been working at George Dickinson's Cark Mills and now were destined to
pull heavy artillery. In the first twelve days of war, 120,000 horses were requisitioned
throughout Britain. Thousands more were to follow. Like the men they served, they
often paid a terrible price.

A cloud of smoke blows away as a gun is tested at the Battery, Silloth. Before the First World War this testing station was run privately by Armstrong and Whitworth, but during the conflict it was taken over by the military. Large guns arrived by rail and were tried out, with whaling harpoon guns said to be among those tested. Shells were fired out to sea, and parties of men went out at low tide to find where they had fallen or had disappeared. The Battery closed in 1928.

It is folklore now, but there is a story about a visiting maharaja who watched a demonstration of fire power and was peeved because the target figures, which were all blown to pieces, seemed to be made out of cardboard or plywood, or so he alleged. Would the guns be any good against *real* people? he wanted to know. Told they most certainly would, he was nonetheless dissatisfied and said he could provide his own targets. 'I have a dozen servants surplus to requirements', he is supposed to have informed the organisers. No account of any resulting massacre is to hand.

Opposite:
Cleator Mill Girls' Football Club line up ready for battle. It is 1917, with many of the menfolk away at war. A case of long skirts, mop caps and plenty of determination to keep things going, in this case on the soccer field. As the men were conscripted into the services, women took on their civilian jobs.

Sitting firmly on his fine steed is Joseph Grisenthwaite, who was sixty when this was taken in 1916. Joseph was a blacksmith at Bowness on Windermere and volunteered for the army in the First World War as an assistant in the Veterinary Service.

A U-boat hunter towers above the minuscule-looking ground crew as it is towed from its hangar. Giant airships grew to be a frequent sight along the Cumbrian coast during the First World War, when they mounted hundreds of convoy and anti submarine patrols. Airship basis were established at Walney Island in the south, and in the north at Luce Bay, west of the Solway Firth in Dumfriesshire, where Windermere photographer Louis Herbert captured graphic scenes like this on official photographic outings.

Great importance was attached to the patrols. In August 1915 a daring German U-boat bombarded the Harrington Coke Ovens Company at Lowca. More than fifty shells were fired at the benzol plant, which was being used in the manufacture of TNT. The works was hit many times, though damage was not severe. The plant was German built so not everyone was surprised by the attack. Another attack took place at Walney where a submarine tried to destroy a hangar with shellfire. Along the coast, in the Irish Sea many ships were torpedoed, but though the German high command admitted later that the airships had curtailed U-boat attacks, the ships were saved in the end by the introduction of the convoy system. U-boats were then forced to seek solo vessels.

Opposite:
Tilting down the sky, His Majesty's Airship No 23 prepares for touchdown. This impressive giant, 535 feet (163m) long, was built at Walney Island, and underwent lift and trim trials in August 1917. She was found to be grossly overweight, due to extra equipment demanded by the Admiralty, and was slimmed down by the removal of cabin furniture and a wireless transmitter generator. Though she flew well enough, No 23 saw little of the First World War, flying mainly in a training role before being scrapped in 1919.

Both of these aircraft were special in their day and were seen frequently over Cumbrian skies. The looming NS II held the world endurance record for airships, for a time at least. And the fighter plane in the foreground, a Bristol, became the class most feared by all but the most skilled German pilots of the First World War. The picture was taken by Windermere photographer Louis Herbert, on one of a number of special photo visits to RNAS Luce Bay across the Solway Firth.

After the war, the NS II — 'NS' for North Sea – achieved temporary fame when it made an epic flight of 105 hours 50 minutes, setting up an endurance record. This lasted until July 1919, when it was beaten by the R34's transatlantic flight. Eventually disaster overtook the NS II, which crashed in a thunderstorm while searching for wartime mines. The crew were killed.

The Bristol F2B fighter came into service in 1917. Initially, attempts were made to fly it as a two-seater, with the rear gunner doing all the shooting. But the crews changed to operating it in a different manner, the pilot using the forward-firing machine gun and the gunner fighting off stern attacks. Large numbers were built and they became one of the most effective aircraft of the First World War. The Bristol continued in service with the peacetime RAF until 1932.

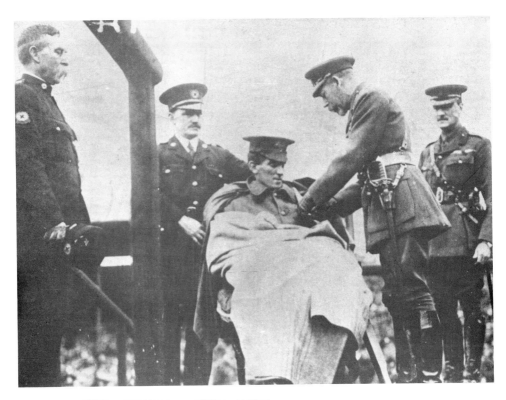

A Victoria Cross was awarded to a First World War air ace, Captain William Leefe Robinson, who was educated at St Bees School from 1909 until 1914. In 1916 William became a national hero after shooting down the first German Zeppelin over England. He saw the war end with the signing of the Armistice in 1918, but died soon after from a flu virus.

Opposite:
First World War hero Private Harry Christian of Ulverston is presented with the Victoria Cross from King George V. Harry, twenty-three, was sheltering in a crater with five other men in front of the British trenches at Cuinchy near La Bassee in 1915. A heavy bombardment began and the group was forced to retreat. Not until they had reached better cover was it discovered that three of the men were missing. Harry returned alone to the crater and found them buried in debris. As shells exploded, he dug the men out and one by one dragged them to safety. A private in the King's Own Royal Regiment (Lancaster), he was awarded the VC for 'most conspicuous bravery' in the face of heavy enemy shell fire. The rescued men all survived the war, and Harry, who is seen in the wheelchair while recovering from malaria, lived to be eighty-two.

A German airship sightseeing as it crosses over Carnforth and heads for southern Lakeland. The trouble was, as the British press was quick to ask, what exactly were the sights they were intent on seeing?

Zeppelin flights over Britain were not new: German airships had been seen enough during the First World War. But this was now the 1930s and the British government of the day was not wholeheartedly enthusiastic about its German visitors.

The Germans sensed this. 'Safety is our only concern', a German officer in Berlin was reported as saying. So that was all right.

Further, the German Air Ministry, in response to alleged flights of the Zeppelin Hindenburg over British industrial complexes, said reassuringly: 'If one of our Zeppelins has *ever* flown low over British industrial territory, then it was only because of consideration of the airship's welfare demanding it.' The ministry also made it clear that passengers who flew in German airships were usually asked to give up any cameras to officers at aerodromes before the flights started, and they were handed back later.

So it was just a case of jolly old sightseeing after all, as the inhabitants of Barrow-in-Furness and its shipbuilding yards were to realise. Likewise Whitehaven, and Workington, and that ammunition depot just across the border. It still wasn't quite 1939.

Time for a Break

IT WAS NOT ALL WORK a century ago, even if to many it often seemed to be that way. Men at least enjoyed some variety. Hunting was widespread and had a good following in rural areas, with numerous hunting packs ranging the fells, hunting mostly on foot. If one did not take part, at least one could watch. Hound trails, football, boxing, and Cumberland and Westmorland wrestling were popular sports, and for the wealthy there was yachting and cricket.

All these aside, though, beer drinking seemed to outdo everything. In England and Wales every Edwardian adult drank on average six pints (3.5l) a week, and drunkenness, though on the decline, was a serious problem. There were six thousand prosecutions weekly, with men the main offenders.

Women were often distinctly unwelcome in pubs. Some landlords painted white lines across the floor at the entrances and women were not allowed to step across them, which is not say that no one tried. For men, though, pubs offered warmth and useful work contacts, as well as places in which to run union branches and sports clubs.

Leisure for the working class was often governed by long working weeks and the scarcity of free time. Lengthmen on the roads might do seventy hours a week; and maids in large houses likewise. Ten-hour days were not unusual for many in farm work, longer in some spots, and at haytime and harvesting they worked all the hours that came. Farmhands were often allowed Saturday nights free to go to a dance, with barn dances especially popular; or an hour or two would be allowed on Sunday to go to church. In general, though, servants looked forward to the half-yearly week-long gaps at Whitsuntide and Martinmas when the hirings were held.

For women who worked in towns, or could get there easily, there was a greater chance of entertainment. In particular, dancing grew to be extremely popular, one small but significant gap in Edwardian uprightness. But even for the maids in town-jobs, a nine or ten o'clock deadline on Saturday night was not unknown, with the master sometimes standing at the gate prominently holding a watch as they came in.

Racing the summer away. These old Windermere Class yachts were one of the great sights of Lakeland. As many as ten at a time would come sweeping along the lake to round the Ferry Buoy and race away, to the delight of many hundreds of spectators who lined the shores. Usually the crew numbered three, the owner and two hired men. Often they were Morecambe Bay fishermen who were brought up to Windermere specially for the season.

The tide is in, and a crowd waits on the jetty at Grange over Sands ready to climb down to one of the yachts and sail out into the wide reaches of Morecambe Bay. At low water it was possible to walk across the bay, and still is, though a guide is essential to avoid the quicksands and the graveyards.

She looks as if she will get a bit hot when stepping out with her hiking staff, but though this young woman's outfit contrasts strongly with those worn today, she was properly dressed for her time.

Their sleeves rolled up, lightweight boots on for the pleasurable trek ahead, this smoking golfing trio poses outside the pavilion, Ambleside. Despite their casual garb there is an air of dandiness, and it surely was hot.

A huge crowd has turned out for the annual Grasmere Sports. The horse-drawn carriages are used as good vantage points, the wrestlers line up distantly. A great day is under way.

The mighty George Steadman, champion Cumberland and Westmorland wrestler, stands proudly alongside some of his trophies. With this glittering display, it will be no great surprise that he was heavyweight champion at Grasmere sports at least fourteen times — some claim seventeen — and had good cause for his pleasant smile of satisfaction.

George was born at Asby, Westmorland, in 1846 and his first win was at Grasmere in 1872 when he collected £8, a fair old sum then. After that he set his sights on the big trophies. He wrestled like a lion, wrote newspaper correspondents. A muscular titan who, once he locked his grip round an opponent, usually won. In his prime George weighed more than eighteen stone (114kg). For thirty years he was heavyweight champion of the world and represented England at international contests.

Lakeland poet Norman Nicholson wrote that, to understand the difference between all-in wrestling and Cumberland and Westmorland wrestling, you almost needed to take part to find out. Many have. Contestants, once they had locked their arms round the other's body, must not let the grip be broken before a fall.

Wrestling venues have included the Melmerby Rounds, the Langwathby Rounds, the old Ferry Hotel, Windermere, the Swifts at Carlisle, the Flan at Ulverston, and of course nowadays, at Grasmere, where the sport thrives in the August gatherings.

All these champions aside, though, time was that many an impromptu wrestling bout took place in Cumbrian farmyards as the hired lads had a good set-to all on their own. It was considered a great treat, and some farmers even gave a prize to the winners. A few champions have likely arisen that way.

Such determined, appraising eyes. Thomas Longmire, like George Steadman, was a formidable Cumberland and Westmorland wrestler. Thomas was landlord of the New Hall Inn, or the Hole in t'Wall, in Bowness, Windermere, and in twenty memorable years he won more than 200 contests.

One of his biggest matches was in September 1857, with the redoubtable Richard Wright of Longtown for the Championship of England Contest. The contest was at the Flan, Ulverston, and some 6,000 people watched. Astonishingly, for five hours the two men struggled to get the first grip and they failed. The match continued the next day but in the end, to the crowd's dismay, it had to be abandoned. The men met again some weeks later, and this time Thomas won. Charles Dickens met Thomas and named him the Quiet Giant. In his own way, Thomas was famous.

The gleaming copper kettle prizes are on display, waiting for someone to win them, the locals are out, and the hound trail is ready for off. Rusland Valley has always enjoyed a good exciting trail.

Before the start, usually two men set off to walk to the distant halfway mark, each with sacking or rags soaked in aniseed and oil. Everything's timed carefully. Then they begin laying the trail from the halfway point, one man dragging the scent round his half of the trail, and one going round the other half, perhaps ten miles (16km) in all, if it's a senior trail. Serious business.

Back at the prize table, as the first man comes back into sight, whoops and yells sound. The eager line of hounds is slipped and off they go. Once the creatures disappear in one direction, the second trail man comes in from the other, completing the circuit.

And then the wait. The anxiety of the trainers increases as they listen for distant hopeful sounds. Another age passes, until there is a sudden shout. A first hound! Then several are in sight. And as they race nearer, an uproar of whistling, bells and yells of encouragement fills the day. The hounds streak across the final field, their trainers going wild. And seconds later the winner is home, panting, pleased, wagging, thirsty, mopping up praise as more whistling sounds for those still racing in. Or not racing in at all, for sometimes a loopy young thing might decide not to turn up until the next day, having set its owner out on a long trail all of his own.

Trail hounds, lighter and faster than fox hounds, can average 20 mph (35kph) over crags, walls and rough ground. Many do.

The prizes — those beautiful copper kettles. They stand in many a Lakeland farm kitchen, reminders of great past wins. But also they stand in some kitchens for quite another reason, for they were a customary gift from grateful households to a loyal servant, usually after seven years.

As to the trails, I once had my own encounter. Down valley from Rusland, at the hamlet of Oxen Park, the dizzier members of a local hound trail mistakenly poured in at my back door, raced excitedly through the cottage living room and belted out at the front. Spilt my tea that day, I did.

Winter fun and games. It is not every day that the river Kent freezes this well in Kendal, but when it does, whether the icy surface looks tricky or not, there are always a few brave souls willing to try out their skates. If the daring ones are few in number, the rest likely enough were hugging their firesides.

A ride on the donkeys on Silecroft beach. Ears alert to every sound, the donkeys await patiently as the little boy, sitting sideways in his box saddle, appears to be yelling that he wants to get off after all.

The ladies and gentlemen of the Black and White Concert Party from Bowness and Windermere are on stage. and ready to present their latest arrangement of songs, dances and sketches, all in aid of charity. Formed by members of the St John Ambulance Brigade, this group gave concerts in many a Lakeland village hall over a period of seven or eight years. And sometimes more happened than expected, as Miss Nora Ballinger (inset picture) remembered vividly ..

'It started out funny from the beginning, really. We set off from Bowness and had hardly gone a little way when we found we'd left our box of costumes behind. Well we had to go back for it and that made us start all late again. We were going to give a concert in the evening, I think, and the roads were that rough a wheel came off and that was something else needed fixing before we got on again. I tell you we were bothered we'd never get there. It was sometime after the Great War, I guess.

Anyway we arrived at the place and we found it hadn't a dressing room — Langdale, I think — so we put a ladder across the corner of the room and hung all our coats on it, and we ladies had to undress behind those coats, stooping down, and we were all undressed ready to put our other things on when the ladder fell down. Well! There was consternation all round, you can be sure! The place was full. Packed, so packed the children had to sit on the front of the platform. There'd be about hundred and fifty there. We struggled to get the ladder up and get dressed. We weren't nude, but it made that concert! It went like a bomb, I can tell you.'

Three light horse-drawn carriages ready for an outing from J W Lee's Kings Arms Hotel, Alston, c1901. While the women's hats are stylish, there are good reasons for the veils. They were not just to anchor one's hat if it grew gusty, they were there to protect one's face from grit flung up off the stony roads. There was usually plenty of competition to get a place in the leading coach.

A fighting cockerel and its owner in northern Cumberland. Cock fighting was once the most popular of the blood sports among Cumbrians, more so even than fox hunting. The fights were a deadly business, the birds, armed with steel or silver spurs, battling ferociously as they set about one another. A fair number of schoolmasters used to enjoy the sport, as well as members of the clergy.

Many villages and hamlets in Lakeland have the remnants of cockpits, though much overgrown. As a sport it was declared illegal in 1835, but it continued, albeit in secret in Lakeland's quietest valleys, for long after that. Many a time the crowd had to run for it in the middle of a *main*, as the battles were called. In High Furness during a talk, I showed a group of people a slide similar to the picture here and unwittingly mentioned that cock fighting no longer took place in Lakeland. A significant pause followed, during which the audience absorbed this useful information. 'Heh, heh, heh!' sounded a deep, knowing chorus.

The first uphill struggle is over, the next has yet to come. The Tinker family and friends from Windermere pause among the slate heaps at the top of Honister Pass during an outing in August 1918. The three-horse charabanc was one of the Lake Hotel coaches from Keswick following the adventurous twenty-two mile (35km) road around Borrowdale, Honister, Buttermere lake and Newlands Pass.

It was one of the most popular Lakeland tourist routes, but it could be rough going, with foot-deep ruts in places. Passengers were often expected to walk up the steepest hills to ease the burden on the poor horses. The weather, too, had to be allowed for. Brollies, in the basket, were often in use, sometimes in strong sunlight, but more usually when raining. Charabanc trips were immensely popular, though women found it hot going walking up the passes in their heavy clothing. This party is about halfway round. A scaring wild road comes next, the descent to Buttermere Lake, then another rough climb up to the summit of Newlands Pass and on down to Keswick. How the Keswick tea rooms were blessed.

An ancient American once complained to me that all his life he had never quite got over the memory of his first Lakeland trip, back in 1910, when he had had to walk over Honister Pass to ease the strain on the horses. 'Young man', he said (I in my twenties, he in his nineties), 'it's the only time in my life I've *paid* to walk.' The recollection still conjured a grim little smile.

Father and son take a motorbike outing in the early 1920s. Cap reversed, Frank Herbert steers and his father Henry sits in the sidecar on a jaunt over Kirkstone Pass. Brotherswater lies distantly and there is not another vehicle in sight. Frank on one occasion managed to tip his father out onto the road when rounding a sharp corner in the Lyth Valley. Both survived and returned home to Windermere and their family photographic business in Bowness with a few light scratches. Frank could not recall his father's remarks.

Opposite:
A mass of capped men has gathered outside the Oddfellows Arms in Caldbeck as the stirrup cup is passed round and the Blencathra hunt prepares to head for the fells. The huntsman John Peel was born and died at Caldbeck and the song that made him famous, *D'ye ken John Peel?* is said to have been sung for the first time in public at the Oddfellows.

Wire wheels and plenty of style, though apparently a bit short of tread on the tyres. This shiny Lanchester pauses on Dunmail Raise during a family outing, perhaps for the photograph, but perhaps also to let everything cool off. The Raise caused many a car to gasp a bit in the old days. A wheel came off my father's own car the day he tried to drive over. The body style here is a full open-fronted landaulette, probably the model known as the 28 horse-power.

Special Events

SPECIAL OCCASIONS TOOK many forms. Sometimes it was just the simple pleasure of an unusual wedding ceremony that drew the crowds, or the arrival of royal visitors, or a travelling theatre putting on a play at the village hall. Stronger stuff and tough talking came with the Suffragette protests, as well as widespread dismay the day an attempt to set up a world speed record on Windermere ended in tragedy.

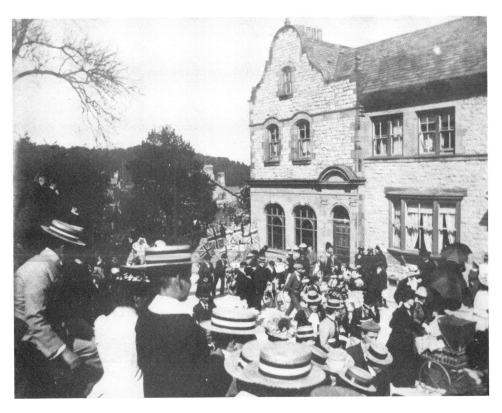

Union flags fly as the people of Grange over Sands parade through the town in jubilation. This was the exciting scene in May 1900, following the news from faraway South Africa, where the Boer War was raging, that Mafeking had at last been relieved. The Boers besieged that town for 217 days in 1899-1900, something that people spoke about in Britain down all the years as one of the most famous of all sieges.

A special occasion at the Moss Grove Hotel, Grasmere, c1900. The hotel was being run by Mr Herman Baldry, who commissioned the picture. His staff are splendidly dressed, and one of the reasons for this gathering was to show would-be guests that the hotel not only had a reliable-looking team, but also a modern wonder, the electric light.

In Edwardian times, many women at first accepted their role as second-class citizens, though not all, and certainly not these Cumbrians, with men allied among them, who are demonstrating in support of women's suffrage, c1911. Cumberland and Westmorland were well represented at the London protests, as the range of banners shows, and this was due in large measure to the remarkable suffragist and pacifist Catherine Marshall, believed to be in the centre of this picture.

Catherine, the daughter of a Harrow school assistant master, lived at Hawse End. Keswick. and spent the best years of her life working for the suffrage movement. She was the organising secretary of Keswick Women's Suffrage Society, setting up meetings across the North, vigorously promoting speakers and spreading leaflets about their aims. But she also championed the cause of First World War refugees, took up cases of conscientious objectors and visited them in prison.

She also campaigned for the Labour party and turned her attention to many other subjects, ranging from women labouring on farms, women in night clubs, training schemes for young widows, and women in munitions work. She proposed using Hawse End as a co-operative community for refugees. It was there that a large collection of her records was found and rescued when the county council bought the building.

In London, the scale of the protest movement can be judged by that of the 17th June 1911, which was some 40,000 strong and stretched nearly five miles (8km).

A wedding is always special, though this one had something a little extra. We may not be able to see the wedding couple, but they were definitely said to be there in the heart of this crush.

Miss Caroline Schultze and Captain Schroder, reported to be Norwegians, were said to want to embark on married life out at sea and could not get their banns called in the normal manner. To ensure that everything was being done properly, a Methodist minister married them out beyond the three-mile (5km) limit on board this sturdy paddle steamer.

It seemed to catch everyone's imagination and this crowd, complete with band, turned out for them at North Pier, Whitehaven, probably in May 1911. As to the wedding vessel, it was built in Liverpool in 1871 for the Hodbarrow Mining Company of Millom and named *Borwick Rails*. In October 1901, the company sold her for scrap, but a shrewd purchaser sold her on for a profit to the Harbour Trust. Eventually she came into the possession of a towing company and, renamed *Ironpolis*, lasted until 1927 when she was broken up.

Cartmel Coronation Band. To the consternation of some, and the delight of others, this much-weathered lady and her street organ were hired specially from Kendal for the coronation festivities of King George V at Cartmel on the 22nd June 1911. As the local almanac recalled later, in 1912:

'The band … caused much merriment at the time, as well as some litigation between the owner and the Railway Company afterwards … The King and Queen were coronated on the 22nd without any hitch … Most of the people in Lower Holker assembled in Holker Park where a substantial Tea was provided, and all sorts of sports and fancy racing competitions. Some people won 2s 6d for the first time in their lives.'

And some heard specially hired street music. Poor old thing.

Opposite:
Royal visitors at Carlisle on the 17th May 1917. A tired-looking King George V takes the salute at Edenside during a troop inspection. Standing behind in a fine plumed hat is Queen Mary. Earlier the king and queen had inspected the shipbuilding yard at Barrow-in-Furness during a wartime morale-boosting tour in the North.

The first wireless message from Caldbeck is ready for transmission on the 4th June 1913. A Lawson from Hesket Hall sent a telegram of congratulation to the high sheriff of Cumberland, Guy P Senhouse, on the installation of the Westmorland and Cumberland Yeomanry.

A white-suited crew member fends off a launch while Sir Henry Segrave sits at the wheel of the streamlined *Miss England II* and waits to set off. It is Friday the 13th June 1930, and the British racing driver is poised to try to break the world motorboat speed record. The idol of millions, Sir Henry already had eight major car-race victories and three land-speed records to his credit. Now, before thousands of spectators, Windermere is the challenge.

With twenty-four instruments to watch, two on-board mechanics were needed, one on either side of Sir Henry. Lining *Miss England II* up on the marker buoys, he applied power to the two supercharged twelve-cylinder Rolls-Royce engines, and within moments the hydroplane was away and streaking down the measured mile.

Turning at the north end of the lake, the craft returned still faster and, as the run neared its end, Sir Henry gave a jubilant thumbs-up signal, realising he had succeeded

Moments from disaster: *Miss England II* races down Windermere at more than 100 miles (160km) an hour. Soon she will flip over and crash.

in breaking the record. No one knows why he decided to do a final run. Turning again, he set off back along Windermere. All seemed well until just before the last marker buoy, then the craft was seen to list and swerve to port. Quickly, it straightened, then swerved to starboard, and again straightened. Moments later the bows come up, the hydroplane left the water, and the craft flipped over backwards and crashed to the surface. One of the two mechanics, Michael Wilcocks, was rescued, badly injured; the other, Vic Halliwell, was killed by a blow to the head. Though Sir Henry was pulled out alive, both his arms were broken, as well as ribs. A thigh was crushed and he had severe head injuries. Anxiously he asked about his mechanics and was told of Halliwell's death; he was told, too, that *Miss England* had broken the record. He died some two and a half hours later.

The craft was recovered from the bed of the lake after two weeks, and it was found that the port side of the hydroplane step was torn and folded backwards. A water-logged branch some three feet (1m) long was pulled from the lake nearby and it bore three gashes. Many believed that this obstruction had caused the disaster.

Miss England's record runs were officially confirmed at a mean speed for two runs of 98.76 miles (158.94km) an hour.

It is May 1935 and the bonfire to commemorate the silver jubilee of King George V is all set, and now there is time for a rest. The horses have hauled this heap by sled to the top of High Pike, Caldbeck, and nightfall is awaited. Gamekeeper Fred Bartle, left, sits it out with two friends. The weather was kind and the blaze a success. The parish magazine reported that 'fireworks and the High Pike bonfire were a jubilant closing to a very memorable day', which included a free tea in Caldbeck parish hall.

The Travelling Theatre has arrived at Rosthwaite village hall. The players, a roving band of young actors and actresses, look casual enough, but they were renowned for hard work, enthusiasm and considerable expertise.

The Travelling Players were formed in 1919 in the aftermath of the First World War. With little money, they set out to bring the arts into everyday life, especially in remote places. They travelled at first in a one-ton lorry, but later in a Lancia, half-car half-bus. Everything was packed in — the players, the scenery and all their baggage. It was a demanding, often exhausting life with a succession of one-night shows, each time packing up and moving on again.

Called officially the Arts League of Service Travelling Theatre, the company gave performances up and down England and Wales for some eighteen years and were a great success. In fact almost too successful.

They visited Lakeland and the surrounding area several times, and were greatly appreciated, though at first a show at Frizington and Cleator Moor proved to be a disconcerting experience. They were invited there to play in 1920 to the miners. While the local population treated them with great kindness, the solidity of the miners in the audience proved unnerving. The founder of the players, actress Eleanor Elder, recalled: 'It transpired it was not the shows that had been unappreciated, but that they made it a point of pride never to applaud or give way to their feelings.'

The programmes, often light-hearted, part variety, part plays, presented works by W B Yeats (*The Land of Heart's Desire*), J M Synge (*Riders to the Sea*), A A Milne (*Wurzel Flummery*), Margaret Cropper (*James Carrick*) and many others, including George Bernard Shaw (prologue to *Arms and the Man*) who gave them strong support. Likewise, Hugh Walpole, living at Brackenburn, Borrowdale, saw them when they appeared at Braithwaite, and was warm in his praise.

In the Lakes, the players' audiences seemed to follow them from venue to venue. Ironically it was their success that contributed to their demise. Amateur dramatic societies flourished in their wake, other little travelling theatres sprang up, and suddenly the travelling players found that their customary venues were already booked by local societies who put on their own productions.

The Travelling Players' spring tour of 1937 was their last. At the end, everything was sold. Sad though the players were, their work was done.

Genuine Fakes?

PICTURES MAY NOT always be what they seem. The ones seen here are sometimes said to be fakes, and that may well be genuinely so.

The Royal Mail near Grasmere appears to be a cut-out of horses and a van imposed on a familiar background. The picture is sometimes believed to have been a commission for Riggs of the Windermere Hotel, which had the mail franchise from Windermere to Keswick. The mail vehicle is said to have been owned by the Royal Mail, while the driver and the horses worked for Riggs. In the original picture, the contrast in tones between the horses and van and their background is more apparent.

Coaches descend Buttermere Hause. An Alfred Pettitt prize-medal series picture which gains in dramatic value, so the cynics claim, by the camera being tilted a little, thus enhancing the steepness of the road. It may be true, though anyone who has been down this particular mountain pass, even today with its modern surface, may wonder why anyone needed to tilt the camera, for the road is steep enough. In some versions of this popular postcard, while the foreground is exactly the same, the poles have been painted out, adding to the wildness of the scene. Or perhaps it was the other way round — the blank scenes had the tilted poles painted in. Or have the poles simply sagged over in the gales?

A thrilling near-miss over Windermere — or yet another fake? If it isn't and the two aircraft really are approaching one another, as appears to be the case, then the crash must have been spectacular.

Captioned *Hydroplanes on Windermere*, the picture originally was produced by Abrahams of Keswick. It has been suggested that both planes are in fact the same aircraft, though you do find some people who say wicked things like that. Whether a fake or not, as a postcard it was a ready seller.

The Daredevils

L AKELAND'S MOUNTAINS HAVE long been a magnet to thousands of walkers and climbers, and to many photographers too. Of course not every crag has a climber dangling on a rope, as the more dramatic pictures here of long ago might seem to suggest — fell walkers now easily outnumber them.

The most courageous mountain man I ever met was a walker. The 1939–45 War had just ended and he came into sight far away along the strath between Cockley Beck and Wrynose pass, a strangely jerking figure who aproached through a jumble of torn up boulders. When we met his awkward gait was explained for he had only one leg and was on crutches. 'Used to climb a lot round here years ago,' he said. 'Gable, Pillar, the Langdales. Up here every weekend! War or no war, I had to see it all again.' Perhaps that is how it has always been with the mountain set. He went off on his crutches, still passionate about the wild side.

Opposite:
Men and women climbers scale the impressive Napes Needle, Great Gable, c1899. Dramatic photographs like this were published widely and the Needle's spectacular outline became an easily recognised symbol, attracting many young bloods to Lakeland's crags.

The Needle was first climbed by the daring Walter Parry Haskett Smith in 1886. Wearing an old tweed suit and nailed boots, he pioneered a route, climbing alone with no special gear, not knowing if he could get to the top or, if he made it, whether he could get down again safely. Feeling, as he confessed, as small as a mouse, the incredibly cool, modest man succeeded in doing both.

Victorian women climbers were pretty courageous, too. In some ways it was harder for them than for men. Living in an age of prudery in which even an ankle had not to show, there was the considerable disadvantage of having to wear long skirts, which meant they could not see where they were placing their feet.

Since Haskett Smith's daring climb, the Needle has been conquered thousands of times, with some six routes to the top. Today his route, the Wasdale Crack, though officially it is designated as Very Difficult (Hard), is regarded by some as only a moderate task. Even so, many climbers speak with respect of those pioneering daredevils who coolly accepted the challenge.

90

In the climbers' pubs and bars of the Lakes, people still call him the Father of English Rock Climbing, and by that they mean Walter Parry Haskett Smith, an Oxford undergraduate who more than anyone is credited with starting off what was to become a major sport in the mountains of Lakeland.

When he was twenty-two, Haskett Smith and a group of friends arrived in Wasdale Head on a fell-tramping holiday, and there by chance they met Frederick Bowring, a veteran walker. Bowring is said to have inspired the young braves, and to have urged them to seek out the more adventurous ways up into the mountains around them. Haskett Smith was deeply impressed, especially by Wasdale, which he had chosen to visit simply by pricking a map with a pin, and he returned the following summer with his brother. Soon they were enthusiastically exploring the heights.

Attracted by a gully, the brothers set off to get to the top and what started as a bit of a scramble turned into a real climb. Eventually they made it and that, albeit a considerably simplified version, is said to be the birth of the great sport in Lakeland. Wasdale Head was to become the centre of Lakeland climbing, and the next couple of decades saw adventurous men pioneering climbs on the central Lakeland cliffs. Alpine climbers apparently did not think much of them, and their climbing techniques were sometimes rated as primitive (there was a shattering disaster in 1903), but even so they conquered some formidable crags which previously had been regarded as unclimbable.

Three great cliffs in particular drew them: the Napes face of Great Gable, Pillar Rock and Scafell Crag. All three helped to teach the new young breed their skills.

Haskett Smith, of course, was not the only climber whose name reminds us of those adventurous days, nor was he and his band the first to climb Lakeland rock. Poet Samuel Taylor Coleridge had climbed down from Scafell summit to Mickledore some eighty years before, and there were numerous others. But when rock climbing began in earnest at Wasdale Head, it was Haskett Smith whose name was to the fore in the 1880s, and Owen Glynne Jones, equally famed, in the 1890s, along with a host of others including the Abraham brothers, renowned for their mountain photographs. For these pioneers it was a time alive with adventure, the young braves seeking out the next foothold into the unknown.

Taking his time, a climber finds a useful ledge while on his way up the rockface, one of many dramatic photographs taken by Mayson's of Keswick.

After twenty-one years of inspired climbing by a growing band of young men, disaster struck in the heart of Lakeland on a blustery Monday in September 1903.

Carefree and adventurous, four friends set out to climb Scafell Pinnacle: R W Broadrick, a Windermere schoolmaster; Stanley Ridsdale of Kew, London; Henry Jupp, of Croydon; and A E W Garrett of Wallington, Surrey. All expert climbers, they spent a challenging morning on Scafell Crag, and in high spirits met up with another group of friends, led by W E Webb, and lunched together on the heights before the two parties turned to different climbs.

The ill-fated four latched on to Scafell Pinnacle, tackling it from Lords Rake. Broadrick led the way, then came Garrett, Ridsdale and Jupp. To this day it is a mystery what exactly happened in the climb that followed.

Webb's party, some 200 yards (180m) away, were finding the going immensely slippery and gusty, and eventually they decided to abandon the climb. No warning of any disaster had been given, and it was as they were leaving that they were horrified to stumble on the bodies of the other climbing party at the foot of the Pinnacle. Of the four, only Ridsdale was alive, though he was in a bad way.

The tombstone in Wasdale Head churchyard in memory of Jupp, Garrett and Ridsdale, three of the four climbers who fell to their deaths in the 1903 tragedy.

In the few hours before he died, he struggled to describe how the tragedy had happened — how Broadrick had complained of being tired, how he and Garrett decided to change positions, how Garrett slipped ...

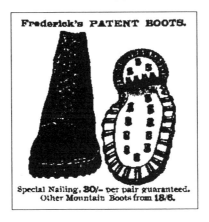

Frederick's PATENT BOOTS.

Special Nailing, 30/- per pair guaranteed.
Other Mountain Boots from 18/6.

Roped up, and definitely concentrating, another daring climber takes to the
heights.

Queueing up for twenty foot (6m) of adventure. Tempting this cheerful party of climbers is Gash Rock in Langstrath, known also as Blea Rock. It is a prominent landmark standing just off the well-worn track to Stake Pass, below Sergeants Crag.

Climbing boots galore. It's Easter 1895 and there is plenty of atmosphere in the entrance hall at the Wastwater Hotel.

The renowned Lakelander Canon Rawnsley, second from the left, supervises the building of the Gough memorial cairn on the summit of Helvellyn, at 3,118 feet (950m). The memorial tells of one of Lakeland's most famous stories.

A young Manchester naturalist, Charles Gough, fell to his death in 1805 when trying to cross with his dog from Patterdale to Wythburn in a hailstorm. But his withered body was not found until three months later above the shores of Red Tarn, and his faithful terrier was guarding it. The dog when found was close to being a skeleton itself and would not allow anyone to come near, and the hounds were set on to catch it.

The dog's deep loyalty touched the hearts of many, and inspired the writing of two poems, *I Climbed the Dark Brow of the Mighty Helvellyn* by Sir Walter Scott, and *Fidelity* by William Wordsworth. Then more than a century ago a woman visitor to Lakeland, Frances Power Cobbe, suggested erecting a monument, and Canon Rawnsley carried the idea through. On a sultry June day in 1891 this simple stone slab was dragged on a horse-drawn sledge to the ridge of the mountain above Striding Edge and set up by the workmen. It records the death of Gough and the faithfulness of the dog, with the closing lines from *Fidelity.*

This sprightly young fellow, Thomas Victor Martindale, was only nine years old when he became lost up in the Lakeland fells. His ordeal was to last for four days and nights.

It was July 1907, and Thomas, whose father was a carter in Penrith, was on holiday at High Howe Farm at the village of Bampton. With a fifteen year old friend, Vickers Bland, Thomas set off to look for a pony which was missing on the hills above the village. They reached a place called White Bog and decided to separate, but to stay within calling distance of one another. Vickers found the pony lying dead in a pool, but by that time thick mist had rolled in and there was no sign of Thomas. In a panic, Vickers went to tell his family and a search party set out in a frantic effort to find the boy.

Thomas had walked on, climbing Helton Fell and eventually coming to a wall, which runs down from High Street. In the mist, he appears to have followed this for miles until he reached Kentmere. It was about three o'clock in the afternoon and he had walked some fourteen miles (22km). He called at a farm to ask how to get back to Bampton, and the farmer, apparently not realising Thomas was lost, directed him back over the lonely Nan Bield pass.

A weary trek ensued and Thomas, engulfed again in mist, turned by error along the high trackless fell between the Kentmere and Troutbeck valleys. That first night he found a hole in the rocks, and huddled inside and slept. On the Wednesday he wandered all day in the mist, foodless and lost. Come nightfall, he slept in among more rocks, and while there a lamb crept in beside him and they kept one another warm. On Thursday, with only water to keep him going, the boy wandered still further, staying that and the following night in a shepherd's hut. Weak from lack of food, on the Saturday he tried another direction, and this time came down Applethwaite Common to a farm at Troutbeck Park, safe at last. A telegram was sent to the police to say that the lost boy had been found.

Thomas had eaten no food for four days. He was dressed as here, in a jacket and knee breeches, but had no coat. The search parties were recalled, and the boy returned home with his father over Hartsop and Kirkstone pass to find that he had become front-page news and a hero of the fells.

A Lakes climbing party of the 1890s. The fifteen members in this group — one or two apparently well corseted — are better equipped for the mountain heights than a first glance reveals.

Few fellwalking expeditions were considered complete without a copy of a treasured Baddeley guidebook as a standby. The traveller's bible was packed with vast amounts of information, from railway timetables to escape routes off the mountains. But this sturdy group has gone one better, for standing on the right is said to be none other than Mountford John Byrde Baddeley himself, guide writer extraordinary.

The famous man lived both in Windermere and in Bowness at various times, and was a tremendous walker. On one occasion he climbed Scafell three times in twenty-four hours to help tend bonfires during Queen Victoria's Jubilee celebrations. So this party of walkers was in good company, and likely enough was walked off its feet.

Baddeley died in 1906 and is buried in the old Bowness cemetery. His famous red-backed volumes opened up the mountain wilds of Lakeland to thousands of people, and indeed seem also to have helped create an entirely new Lakeland mountain, one consisting of a vast and ever-growing number of books extolling the delights and curiosities of the district, a heap to which is added yet one more volume.

Neddy Swainson was not exactly a climber, more of a sportsman-farmer who took the occasional mountain hike. Neddy was born in the hamlet of Nibthwaite, Coniston Water, in 1819, about a couple of months before the advent of the future Queen Victoria. As a young man, Neddy went into carting, carrying copper ore from Coniston down to the canal head at Ulverston where it was shipped out. But the coming of the railway to Coniston wiped out his business, so he started farming at Nibthwaite in 1855. He was an astonishingly active man and his pastimes included following the Ulverston Harriers, even in his nineties. Which brings us to the picture, for it was taken on the 7th July 1914, the day Neddy climbed Coniston Old Man (2,635 feet/803m). With his stock and hunting horn in hand, he posed with his dog by the summit cairn, a mere chicken in his ninety-sixth year.

And that seems a good uplifting place to end this book …

Bibliography

Bradley, A G; *Highways and Byways in the Lake District*; London, 1903.

Bulmer, T (editor); *History, Topography and Directory of Furness and Cartmel*; 1910.

Carruthers, Frank J; *Lore of the Lake Country*; London, 1975.

Clare, T; *Archaeological Sites of the Lake District*; Derbyshire, 1981.

Collingwood, W G; *The Lake Counties*; London, 1932.

Crossland, J Brian; *Looking at Whitehaven*; Whitehaven, 1971.

Denyer, Susan; *Traditional Buildings and Life in the Lake District*; London, 1991.

Elder, Eleanor; *Travelling Players*; Plymouth, 1939.

Fraser, M; *Companion into Lakeland*; London, 1937.

Geddes, R Stanley; *Burlington Blue-Grey*; Barrow, 1975.

Geddling, Evelyn M; *Geddling's Dip*; Hexham, 1987.

Graham, Olivia; *Memoirs of a Lady Motorist*; London, 1916.

Griffin, A H; *A Lakeland Notebook*; London, 1975.

    Inside the Real Lakeland; Preston, 1970.

Hankinson, Alan; *The First Tigers*; London, 1972.

Hardy, Eric; *The Naturalist in Lakeland*; Newton Abbot, 1973.

Hart-Davis, Rupert; *Hugh Walpole*; London, 1952.

Hay, Daniel; *Whitehaven, A Short History*; Whitehaven, 1966.

Jenkinson, H I; *Jenkinson's Practical Guide to the English Lakes*; London, 1872.

Joy, David; *Railways of the Lake Counties*; Yorkshire, 1973.

Kemp, Laurie, and Templeton, Jim; *175 Years of Carlisle*; Runcorn, 1990.

Kirkby, B; *A Collection of Dialect Words and Phrases*; West Yorkshire, 1975.

Lancaster, J Y, and Wattleworth, D R; *The Iron and Steel Industry of West Cumberland*; Workington, 1977.

Lefebure, Molly; *Cumberland Heritage*; London, 1970.

Linder, Leslie; *The Journal of Beatrix Potter from 1881 to 1997*; London, 1966.

Mannix and Whellan; *History, Gazetteer and Directory of Cumberland 1947*.

Marshall, J D; *Old Lakeland, Some Cumbrian Social History*; Plymouth, 1971.

Marshall, J D, and Davies-Shiel, M; *The Lake District at Work*; Newton Abbot, 1971.

   Industrial Archaeology of the Lake Counties; Plymouth, 1969.

Nicholson, Norman; *Greater Lakeland*; London, 1969.

    The Lake District: An Anthology; London, 1977.

    The Lakers; Milnthorpe, 1955.

    Portrait of the Lakes; London, 1963.

    Wednesday Early Closing; London, 1975.

Pevsner, N; *Buildings of England: Cumberland and Westmorland*; London, 1967.

Postlethwaite, John; *Mines and Mining in the English Lake District*; Cumbria, 1975.

Ransome, Arthur; *The Autobiography of Arthur Ransome*; London, 1976.

Rawnsley, Eleanor F; *Canon Rawnsley, An Account of his Life*; Glasgow, 1923.

Rawnsley, H D; *Life and Nature at the English Lakes*; Glasgow, 1902.

Redmayne, W B; *Cumberland Scrapbook*; Carlisle, 1948.

Reed, David W; *Friends' School Wigton 1815-1953*; Carlisle, 1954.

Rice, H A L; *Lake Country Portraits*; London, 1967.

Rollinson, William; *A History of Cumberland and Westmorland*; London, 1978.

   A History of Man in the Lake District; London, 1967.

   The Lake District: Life and Traditions; London, 1996.

Scott, D; *Cumberland and Westmorland*; London, 1920.

Stockdale, J; *Annals of Cartmel*; Whitehaven, 1978.

Wainwright, A; *Pictorial Guides to the Lakeland Fells*; Kendal, 1955-1966.

Wyatt, John; *The Shining Levels*; London, 1973.

Acknowledgements

To the many who have helped --- thank you: for advice, stories, corrections and transport when needed; for the loan of pictures and tracking down some photographs at first only vaguely heard of; thanks, too, to those who arrived unexpectedly at the door with other pictures for possible inclusion. To all mentioned here, and to a number of individuals who wished to remain anonymous, I am greatly indebted for help and permissions.

A number of generous people helped to rescue this book when it seemed it would founder - in particular publisher Daniel Walters of Waltersgill Publishing; Sue and Fred Steinberg of Abraham Photographs; Allan Bowe, general manager, the Oddfellows Arms at Caldbeck; Edwin Rutherford, keeper of social history, Tullie House Museum and Art Gallery; and Colin Smith, author and historian, Bowscale.

My thanks go also to writer Sue Allen, to chief sub-editor David Hay, to Harry and Doreen Knipe and Kathleen and Margaret Ashbridge; photographers Brian Wade and Keith Wilkinson; farmer Nancy Tweddle, and to local studies librarian Stephen White of Carlisle Central Library. Much valuable help came from the writings of author Frank Carruthers who for years produced a wealth of articles for the Cumbrian Newspapers group. A number of the photographs are published for the first time, often coming from private family albums. Any textual errors are my own.

Among the many others who helped are: Simon Abbey, Abbot Hall Art Gallery and Museum, Kendal; Robin Acland, Norman Allonby, Peter Anderson, John Armstrong, Eric Arnison, Thomas Ashburner, P Atkinson, Mary Baxter, Nora Ballinger, Norman Barker, Colin Barr, James Biddall, Winifred Blackadder, Sir Christian Bonington, George Bott, journalist Ross Brewster, Kath Brown, Annie Brownrigg, Malcolm and Colleen, Stephen Cove, The Cumberland News, The Cumberland and Westmorland Herald; Cumbria's libraries, in particular Barrow-in-Furness, Carlisle, Grange-Over-Sands, Kendal, Kirkby Stephen, Millom, Penrith, Silloth, Whitehaven and Workington; Cumbria's records offices at Carlisle, Kendal and Whitehaven; J Day; Whitehaven records office; Muriel Dover, the Dowthwaite Family, Beatrice Earl, Elizabeth Fecitt, E Gaskell, author and photographer Trevor Grahamslaw, the Hadwin Family, J Hardman, Dorothy Harrison, R Harrison, E Heathcote, the Helena Thompson Museum, Workington; the Herbert Family, in particular Frank Herbert, John and Jean Higgins, Alison Holliday, Andrew Hunter, the Rev Joe Isaac, Tommy Jackson, Trevor Jones, the

Kearton Family, Alan Kirkby, Margaret Matthewson, the Mandale Family, the Mann Family, Mayson's, Nils Minor, Mirehouse Historic House, Anne Moffat, Ann Moss, Bill Mossop, Lady Caroline Mustill, Newton Rigg College, writer Denis Perriam, Annie Ramsbottom at Annan Historic Research Centre; Phil Rigby, Cedric Robinson, Mary Satterthwaite, Joan Saul, David Frank Scott, W Scott, the Simpson Family, Colin and Lesley Smith, Margaret Stephenson, Theo Stephenson, the Storey Family, Richard Strike, the Sutton Family, Joan Taylor, Jim Templeton, Malcolm Threlkeld and Family, the Tiffin Family, George Tinker, R Tyson, Robin Walker, Robin Walton, Antoinette Ward, George Whitley, Lyn Whittaker, Fred Wilson, artist Billy Wilkinson, Joanne Wilson and Irene Wren. Thanks to the Pentalk Rural Network co-ordinator Ann Riseman, and its general manager, Ian Huyton, extra photographs came from Jean Bryson, page 40 and Marjorie Wales, page 112, with the additional help of Alison Burbury. Too good to miss.

Index